Saving Grace

NEW HORIZON
PRESS

Dear Reader,

We proudly present the newest addition to our internationally acclaimed true crime series of Real People/ Incredible Stories. These riveting thrillers spotlight men and women who perform extraordinary deeds against tremendous odds: to fight for justice, track down elusive killers, protect the innocent or exonerate the wrongly accused. Their stories, told in their own voices, reveal the untold drama and anguish behind the headlines of those who face horrific realities and find the resiliency to fight back...

In this gripping page-turner, Sarah Brady, a happy, nine-month pregnant mother-to-be is telephoned out of the blue by a woman claiming to have a similar name. When Brady stops by her apartment to retrieve gifts the woman claimed were meant for her, Brady walks into a deadly trap.

Here, for the first time, Sarah Brady tells the whole story of how she fought a deranged, knife-wielding attacker who wanted to steal her unborn child.

The next time you want to read a crackling, suspenseful page-turner, which is also a true account of a real-life hero illustrating the resiliency of the human spirit—look for the New Horizon Press logo.

Sincerely,

Dr. Joan S. Dunphy
Publisher & Editor-in-Chief

Saving Grace

The True Story of a Mother-to-Be, a Deranged Attacker and an Unborn Child

by
Sarah Brady, Patrick Crowley and Eric Deters

New Horizon Press
Far Hills, NJ

New Horizon Press
PO Box 669
Far Hills, NJ 07931

Brady, Sarah, Crowley, Patrick, and Deters, Eric
Saving Grace: *The True Story of a Mother-to-Be, a Deranged Attacker and An Unborn Child*

Cover Design: Wendy Bass
Interior Design: Eileen Turano

Library of Congress Control Number: 2006923964

ISBN 13: 978-0-88282-287-7
ISBN 10: 0-88282-287-X

New Horizon Press books may be purchased in bulk quantities for educational, business, or sales promotional use. For information please write to: New Horizon Press, Special Sales Departments, PO Box 669, Far Hills, NJ 07931 or call 1-800-533-7978.
e-mail: nhp@newhorizonpressbooks.com

www.newhorizonpressbooks.com
Manufactured in the USA

DEDICATION

Life is a precious gift that can be ripped away in mere seconds. Three beautiful souls gave me the will to protect mine. For that I dedicate this book to Scott, and our children.

I love you,
Sarah

Eric Deters and Patrick Crowley dedicate their first book to their wives, for their love and support.

Mary Deters
Pam Crowley

Author's Note

This book is based on the experiences of the authors and reflects their perception of the past, present and future. The personalities, events, actions and conversations portrayed within this story have been taken from memories, interviews, research, court documents, letters, personal papers, press accounts and the memories of some participants.

In an effort to safeguard the privacy of certain people, some individuals' names and identifying characteristics may have been altered. Events involving the characters happened as described. Only minor details may have been changed.

Table of Contents

Prologue

Feb. 10, 2005
Fort Mitchell, Kentucky
Approximately 11 A.M.

The serenity of a suburban midwinter morning shattered when a blood stained, pregnant woman—knife in one hand, telephone in the other—burst into the cold from the small first floor corner apartment in Fort Mitchell, Kentucky.

Screaming and coatless, the woman stopped a very startled gray haired woman driving a red Jeep Cherokee. Nervous about the stranger, the driver only cracked the window.

"Yeah?" is all she could muster to the very pregnant woman, who in response hysterically cried out, "I need help! Please call someone. A woman attacked me. I had to fight her off!"

"There's a police station up the street," the driver stated nonchalantly and drove away.

Flabbergasted, the distressed woman had no choice but to make her way up the sandy hill to Dixie Highway, where the Fort Mitchell Police Station is located. She arrived at the corner of Dixie and Superior, exhausted and out of breath, where she stumbled into the street frantically waving her arms to attract attention.

To her relief, a minivan stopped. The driver, a young mother, had her young daughter with her. The mere sight of the disheveled, wounded woman caused the young girl to cry. Seeing the frightened look on the little girl's face, the woman dropped the knife.

Exhausted, the woman collapsed on a patch of grass alongside the sidewalk. The driver of the minivan, unlike the Cherokee driver, did not hesitate to offer assistance. She asked the collapsed woman if she was okay, asked about her baby and, remarkably calm, explained that she would immediately return to her nearby home and call 911.

Seemingly seconds after the woman left, a male police officer arrived in a cruiser. He exited his car and helped the pregnant woman from the ground to his back seat.

Soon an ambulance arrived. The medics transferred their new patient to the ambulance and initiated medical care. They removed her shirt and began their physical examination. "We're leaving," a medic shouted in urgency to the police officer, "She's going to go into cardiac arrest." As the ambulance sped off, the police officer followed in his cruiser to the hospital.

As they made their way to the hospital, the medics having stabilized her heart, asked their new patient what had happened while simultaneously trying to calm her down. She breathlessly informed them, "A woman in the apartment down the street tried to stab me."

From her position on the gurney, she stared with

tear stained reddened eyes up at the medics who were standing over her, and blurted out,
"She wanted my baby!"

Chapter 1

Growing Up Dirt Poor

With money usually tight, bills would be paid late. Sarah accepted this harsh reality, because she knew poverty from growing up underprivileged. Her family didn't acquire many material possessions. Fortune never blessed her parents with much disposable income. The family had little more than a mutual love for one another and the shirts on their backs.

"We were as poor as dirt," is how Sarah described a childhood seared with memories of evictions, trailer park homes, moving in with relatives and very few toys.

"We were very impoverished," Sarah accepted.

Sarah's sister, Mary Brady, remembers growing up in public housing and living on welfare.

"I've had very few material things all my life," said Mary, who by nineteen had spent half of her life in public Section Eight housing. "I've been a product of the welfare system practically since I was born. I know the embarrassment of food stamps, Medicade and free housing."

"My mother struggled raising four daughters on a minimal income that consisted of pitiful child support payments and the charity of others," Mary said. "However, though there were few luxuries or even necessities, I came from a household that fostered intellectual growth. I was taught that the only way to succeed in the world and escape the oppression of poverty is to receive an education."

"My mother would not accept failure in any aspect of our lives," Mary recalled.

Sarah grew up knowing that vacations were pretty much out of the question, though she remembered a trip to a great aunt's farm when she was ten. The great aunt and her husband had "a lot of money," Sarah recalled. They took her on a trip to Gatlinburg, Tennessee when she was twelve. For those living in Northern Kentucky, Gatlinburg in the Great Smokey Mountains is a popular vacation destination.

Sarah experienced the luxury of going to the movies only once or twice a year. She recalls the excitement of the trips and the magic she was able to enjoy vicariously on the large screen in the theater. Going out to dinner never occurred. In fact, a meal for the entire Brady family sometimes involved little more than sharing one TV dinner. Newport, Kentucky, (where Sarah Brady was born on February 4, 1979 to Connie and William Brady), lies directly across the Ohio River from downtown Cincinnati. In the 1950's, Newport was known to be the Las Vegas of its time. During these years, Newport struggled with its image of sleazy dilapidated strip clubs. A "cleanup" campaign by local activists, federal prosecutors and watchdog reporters drove gambling out of the place once known as Sin City. At one time, mobsters ruled much of the area. However, the "clean up" campaign prevailed and Newport changed direction. By 2005, Newport was able to promote its connection to its past as colorful. Present day restaurants have actually renamed themselves after the "mob" hangouts and bars of the past.

Today, Newport has successfully revitalized itself with a public aquarium, a shopping center and dining complex called Newport on the Levee, and revamped housing. In addition, the city benefitted from a surge in white collar office complexes. Newport is now the gem in the Downtown Cincinnati area for evening entertainment.

As a result of Sarah's father having children from an earlier marriage, and her mother giving birth to a child out of wedlock, Sarah had three half-brothers and a half-sister. Though, this Brady family didn't have much in common with the "Brady Bunch" from the classic television sitcom. Unmarried at the time of Sarah's birth, Sarah's parents wed in March of 1979. Later, they had two additional daughters.

Sarah would remain close to all of her sisters.

Sarah always speaks matter-of-factly and without complaint about her childhood. She is quick to express how much she was loved by her mother, grandmother and sisters. The women in her family have a strong bond with each other. These relationships sustained each of them through very difficult times.

Though she spent most of her life in northern Kentucky, an area of both aging working class neighborhoods and booming affluent suburbs lying across the Ohio River from Cincinnati, Ohio, Sarah also lived briefly as a child in Arizona and Washington. As Sarah's father moved from one job site to another, in order to earn a meager living, his wife and children never experienced formulating ties and security. From her birth until she was two years old, Sarah's family lived in Covington, the Ohio River city. Pursuing work, the Brady's moved to Michigan. Sarah is unable to recall exactly where they lived in Michigan or the exact name of the town.

It would be the first of many relocations for young Sarah.

Sarah's young life was packed with worry, instability and hardship. Her father, an independent carpet-layer, constantly relocated the family out of financial necessity. Sarah's early years are filled with memories of living in several states, constantly changing schools, living in trailers, experiencing embarrassing evictions and having few material possessions and forced evictions.

Few events can cause more heartache and pain for anyone, child or adult, than being put out of your own home. Unfortunately for Sarah, the experience of becoming homeless as a child proved commonplace.

Despite their harsh living conditions, Sarah's mother provided love and grounding, while her father was absent. Even when he was around, he spent little time with Sarah. Sarah feels he didn't tend to her emotional needs and didn't live up to his parental responsibilities.

Sarah describes herself as a quiet, yet independent child, traits undoubtedly developed from spending her formative years being the new kid in school and not having the foundation of a two-parent home.

Despite the hardship, Sarah succeeded academically and enjoyed learning. The classroom provided a measure of stability not often found in her home. In fact, her studies allowed Sarah to escape from the sad realities of her life. She took advantage of the opportunity.

"I loved school," she remembered. "I did well in school."

In Michigan, the family lived in a trailer on a small piece of land that Sarah's father had bought. Sarah remembers a log cabin he built on the property. A photograph from the time shows two-year-old Sarah with short, dark hair wearing a nightgown and standing alongside a green and white trailer and a one-room cabin that could hardly accommodate even a family.

Soon after arriving in Michigan, the family moved again. Sarah's father could no longer afford the property and sold it.

The family returned from Michigan to Covington, Kentucky living on Scott Street, a long north-south corridor that leads from the Ohio River into the heart of the city. Sarah also recalls living in her grandmother's house before she began formal schooling. Covington divides the public school into districts. Children living on and off Scott Street attended the Glen O'Swing school.

Sarah's attendance at that school was quite short. By the time Sarah began first grade, the family moved to a trailer park in South Covington. The trailer park had an infamous reputation. It was located in the middle of four earthen walls which created a square. It had the appearance of a fort. The walls exceeded the height of the trailers giving a "pit" appearance. Police didn't bother to venture into the trailer park. Today, it no longer exists, having been overrun with commercial development next to an interstate highway.

"I don't remember what it was called," Sarah said years later. "I just remember it was dirty."

After living in the filthy trailer park, the family moved to another trailer park in Ryland Heights, a small community in the country. Unpretentious by nature and grateful for any small luxury, Sarah felt this trailer park was much nicer than the one her family previously lived in. Ryland Heights, a beautiful area along the Licking River has scenic views, an abundance of velvety green trees and fresh air. The Licking River joins the Ohio River at Downtown Cincinnati and Northern Kentucky. It splits Kenton and Campbell counties and the cities of Covington and Newport. The Rockwellian community of Ryland Heights Country Club is also in the area. It is not a posh place, but a warm and picturesque community nested in a flat area against a mountain. Every season brings its own special charm.

"We had a really nice double-wide trailer, similar to the newer ones," Sarah wistfully recalls. However, hard times forced the family to move again after just four months.

"I missed that lovely community and walking outside among the beautiful trees and flowers," Sarah recalled wistfully.

As Sarah recounts her family history, one concludes Dickens could have written some of the pitiful events and circumstances she experienced as a child. But, she maintained a sense of pride and dignity. The words "trailer park trash" are part of our common language. In reality, it is unfair to stigmatize anyone who must or chooses to live in a trailer or trailer park. The labeling is cruel and unfair. The television series, "My Name is Earl" does a terrific job of making lighthearted fun at "trash." Eminem, through his music and movie, proudly and defiantly embraces the reality of growing up in such a setting. Regardless, Sarah gained resilience and strength though she bounced from one trailer park to another.

After the Michigan-back-to-Kentucky debacle, Sarah's father moved the family to Phoenix, Arizona, trying to find work as a carpet layer in the fast-growing southwest.

In Arizona, the family stayed with her father's brother, also a carpet layer, who provided the dwelling in which they stayed.

Sarah describes the home as either a cottage or a refinished garage with just three rooms—living room, kitchen and bathroom. They lived without furniture and without air conditioning in the sweltering heat of the Arizona summer. The family slept on the floor.

Only a few months after this move, Sarah's father had a falling out with his brother. The family moved to the north outside of Seattle, Washington. This time the beleaguered family rented a camper home.

One day, just a few months after the family arrived in Seattle, Sarah recalls a man stopping by and informing the family that they needed to leave. Even at a young age, Sarah sadly became accustomed to the family losing their homes. She understood what the man wanted and why he was there. The purpose of his visit was to repossess the van. Apparently, the sight of the children living in such cramped quarters moved the man toward momentary compassion.

"The guy should have taken the van right then and there," Sarah recalled. "But he looked at my dad, looked at us, and allowed us to leave in the morning."

The family fled in the middle of the night, enduring the long cross country trip all the way back to Covington where they moved in with Sarah's grandmother. They were in a desperate situation at the time. At this point, the several moves had begun to take a heavy toll on everyone in the family.

Sarah's grandmother lived on Madison Avenue, the main north-south corridor through Covington that stretched from its booming river front through aging residential neighborhoods, past empty storefronts and vacant buildings that gave way to newer strip centers, and finally to the subdivisions sprouting up in the far south end of the city. Madison Avenue ran parallel with Scott Street, one block over, where Sarah previously lived until the age of two years old. Unable to afford a place of their own, they remained with her grandmother, nearly a year. They eventually were able to move just a few houses down the street to the second floor of a two-family home. Holmes High School, the city's public high school that Sarah would eventually graduate from with honors, was also down the street. German Town Pizza, a popular neighborhood restaurant named for the many German immigrants who settled in Covington during the city's early years, and the Ameristop convenience store where Scott's mother would eventually work, were both located nearby.

"We never remained anywhere for long unless we were with grandma and when we went there I wished we could stay, " Sarah said wistfully.

Sarah was about eight years old when she moved again to a two-family home. After so many relocations, many other memories become blurred, but Sarah clearly recalls her mother and father disagreed more and more vehemently during this period.

Both Sarah's education and Mrs. Brady's taking a stand against her husband were factors that caused the marriage to falter. Sarah felt responsible. It was a heavy burden for a young child to bear.

As Sarah prepared to enter the fourth grade, her parents' marriage was disintegrating. The school contacted Sarah's mother, informing her that administrators believed Sarah should change schools to attend advanced classes at Latonia Elementary. Sarah, they told the very proud mother, was a gifted child who needed the challenge of advanced classes.

Unfortunately, her father resisted.

"Absolutely not," Sarah's father said. "I've told you before. A woman's place is at home. She needs to learn to cook and sew and that's all."

Even as a child, Sarah knew the error of her father's opinion. She loved school and in each one gained a reputation as a good student despite almost yearly school transfers as a result of the frequent family moves. Her favorite books were from the *Little House on the Prairie* and the *American Girl* collections. The adventures of Laura Ingalls on the plains and the various historical characters enthralled and fed Sarah's imagination and took her far away from the starkness and bareness of her environment. The stories transported Sarah out of her deprived world and into a better place. Sarah's mother always found a way to purchase one of the books, and Sarah and her sisters would share the book until they each read the story and talked and laughed as they shared the adventure together.

Also, given the family's financial circumstances, school held greater significance to Sarah. She wanted to take advantage of the opportunity, but her own father stood in the way.

"I was just ten. I already knew from his telling me again and again that my father believed women should stay home, take care of the kids, cook and clean," she said. He possessed the chauvinistic "barefoot, pregnant and in the kitchen" attitude.

But Sarah's mother decided to take action. She didn't want her daughter living the kind of life which cursed her: moving constantly, never having enough money to settle down, the constant worry about where the family would live, and the fear of not being able to put food on the table for her children.

She knew Sarah had a promising future. Sarah had proved bright, strong and able to the handle the constant upheavals in a transient existence. Sarah's education could be her ticket to a better way of life. Mrs. Brady refused to allow Mr. Brady to hinder Sarah's future. He had already caused plenty of problems.

"My mom stood up to my dad," Sarah said. "She told

me she didn't want me having to live the way she did. I'll never forget that. She was a strong woman who made us feel loved and valued."

The fight over Sarah's education proved to be the last of many arguments between her parents. Sarah was a quiet, introverted child. Therefore, she never outwardly showed the effects of her father's disdain for her education. Many of the fights between her parents were over Sarah and how she was to be raised.

Sarah's mother decided she wasn't going to subject the children to the conservative outmoded attitude of her husband. Mrs. Brady knew an education would be her daughter's ticket out of poverty. Connie felt so strongly about the importance of Sarah's future that she packed her personal belongings, gathered up her girls and left her husband to move in with Sarah's maternal grandmother.

"When we lived with my grandma," Sarah would later recall, "it was me, my three sisters and my mom in one room for seven years."

"My parents split when I was ten, but they lived separate lives for a long time before the divorce was final," Sarah recalled. "I mean, there wasn't a relationship between my mother and father." Many lucky girls know the special relationship and bond with fathers which leads to the expression "Daddy's girl." The familial bonds of father-son, father-daughter, mother-son, mother-daughter, forges either happiness or disappointment. Sarah had to learn to live without the unconditional love of her father. Thankfully, she was blessed with this kind of love from her mother.

Sarah's at a loss to explain her father's lack of

attention when she was a small child. Regardless, Sarah remembers an almost complete emotional disconnect from her father. Maybe it was because he was already married when he struck up a relationship with Sarah's mother, and the couple wasn't married until after Sarah was born. Maybe, she sometimes wondered, he looked at Sarah as the source of his own troubles. Maybe his difficulty in earning a living for them usurped all his time and effort.

"He was never close to me, ever," Sarah said. Her father stood about five-foot-ten, weighed one hundred seventy-five pounds and had droopy blue eyes. White hair covered his scalp, and he often wore a beard.

For a long time Sarah couldn't, or more appropriately wouldn't, refresh the memory of her father by even looking at a picture of him from those days. She preferred to leave it all behind and avoid reminding herself of what might have been and should have been.

Nevertheless, Sarah has fond memories of her mother's strength and love. What Sarah's mother couldn't provide in the manner of money, material goods and a stable living environment, she made up for in providing her daughters with the attention they deserved.

Sarah's mother always accompanied the girls to school, even when other kids had to make their way alone.

"She never let us walk to school without her," she said. "She was a good mom, a very good mom," a testament that money is not the only source of happiness.

But as a single mom without an education and without formal job training, the family was mired in a cycle of poverty that seemed too impossible to escape. The only jobs available paid minimum wage and failed to generate enough money to pay daycare for her four children.

Sarah's mother had difficulty obtaining public assistance, because at that point, she lived with her mother. Thankfully, food stamps and a medical card helped the family get some decent food and care.

"We didn't always have what we needed or would have liked, but as a single mother she worked hard to take care of four kids; and it was really tough," Sarah shook her head.

Living at grandmas' was crowded. Grandma, Sarah's mother, Sarah and her three sisters shared the two-bedroom house for seven years. The children never had rooms of their own but slept with their mother. Somehow they managed to share this small space and feel loved.

As always, money remained tight. Mr. Brady only contributed the fifty dollars a week in child support ordered under the divorce decree.

A "big time thing," as Sarah recalls it, was playing imaginary games with her sisters. Sarah's mother bought pieces of fabric and the girls played dress-up. They drew pictures with crayons and watched a few television shows. Like most little girls, Sarah and her sisters loved Barbie dolls. They envied one little girl who lived in the neighborhood who owned an entire box of Barbie Dolls with all the accessories and dresses. When Sarah's mother was able to, she bought her girls'

Barbie dolls at the only place she could afford, the local Dollar Store.

The family never went hungry, but there were some pretty sparse meals.

"My mom always made sure we ate, but sometimes it would come down to the four of us sharing one frozen pizza. We had to do with tiny portions of food while our stomachs growled."

Even now Sarah tries to make the best of a tough situation, explaining but not complaining about the circumstances.

"I'm not really a big eater," she said, as if still speaking to her mother and grandmother.

Growing up, Sarah and her sisters were rarely able to enjoy the chance to revel in the joyous childhood fantasy of Santa Claus. Sarah and her siblings wondered why they were left out; all the other children in the neighborhood received visits and presents from Santa. Santa visited the little girl down the street who proudly owned nearly one hundred Barbie dolls, but most years he and his reindeer failed to pay a visit to the Brady rooftop on Christmas Eve.

Sarah's mother, Connie Brady, explained their family was simply too poor to afford any presents.

So while other children opened their piles of gifts on blessed Christmas mornings, the Brady girls received a cookie in a stocking, maybe five dollars in the form of McDonald's gift certificates, socks, underwear, and if they were lucky, one or two toys from the Dollar Store.

Aunts and uncles sometimes intervened with a few small toys to ease the pain inflicted on their nieces by the absence of gifts at Christmas. Despite it all, Sarah always knew her mother cared and did her best to support the family. Deprivation was quite simply just the way it was in her world.

Sarah appreciates all her family did and tried to do for the holidays. Dinner with her aunt and uncles always made the season a little more cheerful. She was even thankful for the gift of an orange from her grandmother.

"I guessed back in her day an orange was a big deal and I knew it was a gift of love. That meant more to me than any big gift could."

"I knew my mother and grandmother tried to do their utmost to make a hard life a little easier for me and my sisters not only on holidays but every day."

Chapter 2

High School Sweethearts

Sarah's life began to look brighter once she began classes at Holmes High School. Money was still a problem, but soon school, enjoyable activities, friends and classes kept her mind occupied and focused.

She blossomed into a lovely young lady. Sarah made the honor roll in advanced classes, ran cross country, played a year of indoor soccer and made the cheerleading squad all four years. Her peers chose her as homecoming queen her senior year and she graduated in 1997.

To her mother's and her own credit, Sarah's upbringing never resulted in Sarah becoming a "wild child" in high school. In fact, she describes herself as a little naive.

"I cheered with a group of girls and I listened to them talking about parties, sneaking out of the house and doing this and that with boys. I mean, yeah, I liked boys, but not to that extent."

Sarah dated a few boys at the beginning of high school, but no serious relationships developed. She never had a steady boyfriend until she met Scott. Sarah Brady and Scott Hatton went out for the first time in February of Sarah's junior year. She and Scott hung out with a group of mutual friends who went to movies, attended games and partied together. Scott already had a son. His son was ten months old when Sarah and Scott started dating. Scott, who was only sixteen when he learned he was going to be a father, was no longer involved with his son's mother.

Despite Scott's spending as much time as he could with his son, Sarah and Scott appeared to be idyllic high school sweethearts. He was a popular and accomplished athlete; she was a pretty cheerleader. She cheered at Scott's football games in the fall and his basketball games in the winter. She watched him play baseball in the spring and summer.

Besides being involved in sports and cheerleading, when Scott wasn't seeing his son, Scott and Sarah spent their free time like many American teenagers—they bowled, saw movies together or attended parties and summer festivals with a large group. Both of their families had little money, though Scott's family was financially better off than Sarah's.

Sadly, Sarah has none of the material remembrances of her high school years—yearbook, class ring or senior pictures.

"Couldn't afford them," she confessed.

Scott's family lived in a neighborhood like much of Covington, a place of older homes, rental properties, corner bars and working class families. Scott wasn't ashamed of where he lived. But he played summer baseball with boys from out in the suburbs who lived in $300,000 and $400,000 homes. Whenever one of those kids picked him up for a game, Scott's father drove him to another part of Covington so the kids didn't see where Scott lived.

"We didn't have anything like the other guys on the team, and I guess it bothered my dad," he said.

An all-around athlete and an exceptional baseball player, during his senior year in high school, according to the *Kentucky Post,* he had been named an All Star shortstop by the Northern Kentucky Baseball Coaches Association. Scott graduated as one of the leading hitters in school history and attended Wright State University in Dayton, Ohio, for two years on a baseball scholarship.

Anyone with a knowledge of baseball is aware of the physical skill required to play the position of shortstop. Scott played the position with exceptional results.

In baseball, Scott set most of the hitting records at Holmes and led the team to one of its best seasons ever and accepted a baseball scholarship to Wright State, fifty miles to the north in Dayton, Ohio. Dayton is the home of the Wright Brothers, the famous brothers first in successful piloted flight. Scott was also offered a scholarship to attend Kent State University near Cleveland in northeastern Ohio.

After graduating high school, Sarah stayed in Covington, taking a customer service job with Star Bank. She enrolled at Northern Kentucky University, a state college in Highland Heights, Kentucky, not far from Covington.

"I went to night school one semester while I was working," she said. "I didn't have a car, I didn't drive. I couldn't begin working full time and going to school and taking the bus."

Throughout Scott's freshman year in college, Sarah was able to see him two to three times per month. She didn't drive, so Scott's parents took her to Dayton so she could spend the weekend with Scott and watch him play baseball. Scott would bring her home on Sunday nights.

During this period, Sarah grew close to Scott's parents. His father lacked a college education, but he held a solid job working third shift at a printing company across the river in Ohio. He worked his way up the ladder and supported his family with his earnings. Scott's mother worked at a local convenience store. Sarah spent time at their house even during the college year, but she especially enjoyed the summer when school was out, a time she looked forward to when she and Scott could spend more time together.

Soon, Sarah moved in with a friend and her parents in a neighborhood known as Wallace Woods. It is Covington's finest and still boasts sprawling turn-of-the-century homes and apartment buildings. Sarah and her friend rented the upstairs, paying forty dollars a week for a living room, kitchen, bedroom and bathroom.

Scott returned to Wright State for his sophomore year. But after coming home shortly following Christmas, he caught a bad cold. He called the school to inform them he needed to take a week off due to illness. Watching his down spirits, Sarah knew something more than being sick was troubling him.

Shortly after making the call, he confessed to Sarah he did not want to return to school at all.

"I miss my son; I miss being at home," Scott told her. "I'm afraid I'm going to miss out on his T-ball games and baseball games. And you can never make up for missing things like that with your child."

Sarah remained understanding even though Scott gave up his scholarship, his education and his chance to continue playing baseball. However, her support did not imply that she felt giving up a college education was a good decision. Sarah was well aware of the lifetime benefits gained from such an education. Regardless, she did not judge.

"He's a very good dad," she explained. "Even when he was sixteen and broke up with his son's mom, he made a very mature decision. He didn't want to be with her, but he wanted to take raise his son and be a good father."

Scott and the boy's mother eventually worked out their differences regarding their parental rights and duties, and agreed to have joint custody of their son. The boy's mother married and considers Sarah a very close friend.

Through high school, Scott attracted some interest from professional baseball scouts. Looking back he knows he never would have lasted playing minor league baseball away from northern Kentucky, his son and the young woman he loved.

However, now being over the reality of having left college and put aside his dream of playing professional baseball meant Scott had to find a different lifestyle and career. Once Scott left school he moved in with his parents. Sarah moved in as well. She continued working at the bank, while Scott picked up odd jobs part-time.

But it was difficult for Scott to find full time work, as well as his place in life.

"Scott never held a steady forty hour per week job until he was in his early twenties," Sarah gives in a candid and blunt assessment. "He didn't know what he wanted to do, and he was a little immature about working."

Scott's family wasn't well off, unlike Sarah though, the children in the family were not aware of the fact that they were poor. Scott's parents gave him money if he wanted new clothes, a new pair of shoes or money to take Sarah on a date. Scott played on a traveling baseball squad that required money from each member of the team. Scott's family paid a large sum of money so Scott could play baseball. Sarah's father had made no such sacrifices for her.

Scott's parents' generosity was foreign to Sarah. Sarah experienced poverty for so long that after working and earning money, she held onto it.

She had grown up without money so that when she had it and was earning it, she knew how to save it.

"He lived a totally different lifestyle than I did," Sarah said. "He would ask his mom for thirty dollars to take me to the movies, and she would give it to him. Thirty dollars paid for a week's worth of food in my family. There was no way to compare our upbringing.

Sarah went on, "Scott's family didn't have a ton of money but they remained comfortable. The kids could have what all other kids in our class had. They wore clothes that were in fashion and went to restaurants and movies."

For a long time Scott had no idea about Sarah's family financial woes. Sarah kept him in the dark about how she was raised and how she lived.

"Since I had my own job, I hid from Scott the fact that my family was poor for about two years," Sarah said.

Sarah had realized at an early age that if she wanted spending money she needed to work. So every summer, from age fifteen to eighteen, Sarah worked the concession stand at Softball City, a hilltop sports complex in Covington. Softball City contained four softball fields and a concession stand in the middle. The complex held title as the most popular softball venue in northern Kentucky. Sarah dispensed all the beer and hot dogs softball players and fans could drink and eat.

"I saved up my money for the months that I wasn't working so I would have money all year round."

Sarah paid her own cheerleading fees and paid for her uniform. She also paid for cheerleading camp. She bought her own clothes as well.

"I just knew that once I had a job my expenses became my responsibility."

In Sarah's home, there was little living room furniture, only a few plastic chairs and a sofa which was a bench covered with an old fabric, and to create colorful decor a few throw pillows were scattered up against a wall. A twenty inch television sat on a small table. The kitchen table consisted of a wooden picnic table and benches. Sarah and her sister slept in bunk beds until her senior year when her grandma bought her a twin bed.

At times, Sarah's family had the luxury of cable television, but it was often turned off for nonpayment. The family suffered the same problem with their phone. Many times Sarah's family failed to pay the bill and the phone company responded by disconnecting the service. Sarah's grandma always came through to pay the phone bill so the service would be reconnected and they would be able to speak.

Scott's lack of full time employment sometimes frustrated Sarah. After leaving Wright State, Scott primarily worked seasonal jobs. He began employment with a lawn treatment company where he remained for two years. However, when the weather turned cold, the work and the paychecks stopped. Like the concrete business, lawn treatment work is fickle and depends on the weather.

"He was off for almost six months, and did nothing," she said.

Sarah, meanwhile, continued working full time in banking, first in customer service and later in collections. However, collection work made her uneasy, because her own family faced dire financial circumstances so many times. Though her faith was strong, she took no comfort in knowing that Saint Matthew allegedly collected taxes and still wrote part of the Gospel.

At home things stabilized somewhat; Sarah and Scott eventually moved out of Scott's parents' house into a four-bedroom house in Florence, Kentucky, a suburb bisected by Interstate 75 about ten miles south of Covington. Florence has one of the highest concentrations of retail and restaurant establishments in the country. The centerpiece of this development is the Florence Mall, which in the 1970s had been one of the region's first major shopping malls.

Florence was very different from the other places Sarah had called home. It was an area known for its comfortable subdivisions, newer ranch and bi-level homes, minivans and SUV filled driveways, family cookouts and neighborhood gatherings that took place on ample and polished decks and on closely cut suburban lawns.

Sarah thought it was a great area and she was thankful to live in a place that she could someday raise a family with Scott.

But Scott and Sarah's stay in Florence was hardly full of suburban bliss.

Their rent was $1,000 a month. To cut down on costs, Scott's brother and his girlfriend also moved in. Scott's father, who had recently separated from Scott's mother, helped his sons by paying part of the rent.

But their good fortunes didn't last. Scott's brother found part-time work; his girlfriend and Scott weren't able to find jobs at all. Sarah found herself the only person in the house with a full-time job, but she only brought home less than $1,000 every two weeks.

After four months, the tension of sharing a home with three unemployed roommates took its toll on Sarah. She left and moved back in with her mom. At that point, worried and disappointed, she also decided to break up with Scott.

"I was stressed out," Sarah said. "I'd been poor all

my life, but was not going to live with no one else working but Scott's brother and I. There was no way I could take care of all the bills."

But living without Scott was just as miserable. A few months later Sarah and Scott reconciled. They moved to an apartment on Catalpa Street, once again near Holmes and across from a well-known local chili parlor. Saving their money less than a year later, they moved to Denver Street, which is in the same Covington neighborhood, and remained there for three years. Eventually they rented a house near a Covington neighborhood known as Latonia.

Latonia was the first "suburb" of Covington, a large collect-tion of small brick homes and neighborhood business districts developed in the years prior to World War II. The community boasted public and parochial schools, corner grocery stores, neighborhood bars, family-owned restaurants and an American Legion Hall. The town had seen better days, a victim of residents fleeing for newer subdivisions and suburbs outside of Covington, but is still not a bad place to live, particularly for a young couple starting out. The homes were affordable and the streets were loaded with families and kids.

For the first time planned, Sarah and Scott also took a few trips to Disney World and to North Carolina, for his son's out-of-town basketball tournaments. But even though they bought tickets to Disney World, they never made it to the park.

For a while, "survival 101" was how Sarah described her relationship with Scott. As with any relationship, Sarah and Scott experienced difficulties. They fought about money, about Sarah's relationship with his son's mom and other issues that sometimes took a while to solve. They became engaged during Christmas of 2002, but never set a wedding date. Both have admitted some fear about making such a deep and lasting commitment, especially with their parents' history of divorce and observing so many of their friends marry and divorce. "Of all of our close friends, Scott and I have been together longer than anybody we know. We've made it through all the hard times when all these other people have fights blow up," Sarah boasts.

Although they often talked of having the family they both wanted, they were somewhat fearful not only because of their strained finances but because doctors advised Sarah she could not conceive.

"They pretty much told me, you're probably not going to have kids," Sarah said. "If it hasn't happened by now, it's probably not going to happen."

Nevertheless, over the years, hope stayed in the back of her mind and Sarah estimates taking many home pregnancy tests. Each one turned up negative.

But in June 2004 Sarah began feeling ill, almost like she was experiencing a strange flu bug from which she couldn't seem to wholly recover. She chalked it up to P.M.S.

Chapter 3

Expectations

Then one weekend, Sarah and Scott had traveled to Bloomington, Indiana, to watch his son play in a basketball tournament. Not only were Saturday and Sunday rainy and stormy, but Sarah felt awful.

A queasy stomach kept her in the hotel bathroom. Her scheduled period never arrived, though that wasn't unusual for Sarah since she had a history of irregular menstruation.

However, when she continued to feel really sick she called to her boyfriend. "Scott," she told him, "something is wrong with me." She described her symptoms. Later Scott figured out what Sarah implied by "something."

Watching her clutch at her stomach after returning to Kentucky on Sunday, Scott recommended she take a pregnancy test if she thought she possibly could be expecting a child.

"But don't worry if it comes up negative," he said

comfortingly.

Scott's mother took Sarah to the grocery store. The only pregnancy tests in stock were not the best quality. They only cost about a dollar. "Probably not very reliable," Sarah mumbled. But she bought two anyway and they left after her mom had made her purchases.

Once they were home, Sarah quietly and without any announcement went into the bathroom to take the test. Her house was crowded that day for a family gathering.

Thirty seconds later, Sarah sat on the closed toilet seat and just stared at the result.

It read positive.

"That can't be right," she murmured. So she used the second test.

Same result.

She began to weep. Walking past the bathroom, Scott overheard her crying and asked what was wrong. Sarah called, "Come in," and handed him one of the tests.

He just looked at it. "What does it mean?"

"That says I'm pregnant," Sarah told Scott. "I don't know whether to be happy or afraid. We can't afford a child now."

Sarah was visibly upset.

Scott's son was nearly nine years old and needed their financial support. Sarah had helped raise him since he was ten months old and watched him grow into a spirited young boy. Sarah, and especially Scott, had been very active in his son's life, particularly his sports.

For the first time in three years, Scott was working a steady construction job, but was the job secure and would it last? Sarah made nearly $50,000 per year working in mortgage collections for Provident Bank in Cincinnati.

The idea of a baby, though wondrous, also seemed intimidating. How would they manage? She didn't know whether to be happy or miserable.

The turn of events equally upset Scott, but Sarah couldn't discern if Scott's emotion was a result of the news or because the house was full of family and friends downstairs who could hear Sarah crying.

It wasn't long until the family in the house began asking what was happening. Scott wanted to keep the news between Sarah and him, but she blurted out that she was pregnant to Scott's mom.

Looking back, Scott and Sarah realize they were really upset about the financial ramifications of having a child when they were just becoming able to support themselves and Scott's son. Having had to face all those people at the time Sarah had just gotten the results of the pregnancy test made them more nervous.

"Scott said he became uptight because discovering you're having a child is a personal thing between two people. He says now that the announcement should have been kept between him and me until we had time to share our feelings," Sarah said. "But it was like boom, all these people were all there at the same time and there was no time to talk about us."

After that first stressful night, Sarah and Scott knew down deep both were really happy about the event and began celebrating and planning for the birth of their child. Sarah visited with her OB/GYN doctor to confirm the results of the test and discuss the morning sickness she was experiencing.

"I was nauseous almost every day the first two or three months. I lost eight or ten pounds."

Scott and Sarah worried about the effect the weight loss might have on the baby, but the doctor assured them their child was fine. She eventually began putting on weight. Sarah gained a total of about thirty pounds, which her doctor felt was normal and healthy.

"Still I'd never been so emotional. I was tired all of the time and I was cranky. I couldn't relate to women who say it feels so great to be pregnant. I couldn't identify with that, but I did look forward to having our child."

It is a common admonishment that anything worth having requires great sacrifice. Sarah felt that considering the great gift of life a child brings, motherhood, in which a woman endures so much on the path to delivery, is certainly an example of that truism.

As Sarah's due date of early February 2005 drew closer, she and Scott became more concerned with how his son would handle having a sibling. Though he already had a half-brother and half-sister, for all intents and purposes he was an only child to Scott and Sarah.

Sarah felt that the three of them were a family, and as a result of her own deprived childhood, Sarah admittedly spoiled Scott's son a little. He was also very used to spending a lot of time with Scott.

"I try to compensate for the things I didn't have," Sarah explained. "I spoil him and buy him whatever he wants."

Sarah and Scott spent some time talking to his son about his new brother or sister. To their surprise he handled it well and expressed no concerns about not being the center of attention when the baby arrived.

In fact, Scott's son was so comfortable with the situation that Sarah suggested he go along when the doctor determined the sex of the baby.

"I want him to be part of this," Sarah told Scott, "I want him to feel it; I want him to know that this baby is going to be a part of him too."

It was no surprise that the boy wanted a little brother.

Shortly after arriving at the doctor's office on the day of the ultrasound, the nurses hooked Sarah up to the machine. Her stepson, as most young boys would do when they are bored, began to fiddle with the room full of sensitive equipment and delicate instruments.

He was standing on the scale when the doctor saw him.

"I think you're going to have a baby sister," she said.

"Are you kidding me?" he responded. "It's not a boy? Can you check and make sure."

"Honey," the doctor said, "it's a girl."

"Oh well, that's still good. Even a sister can be fun."

Throughout the rest of Sarah's pregnancy, Scott's son was quick with advice, though still a trifle disappointed that he wasn't going to have a little brother. Nevertheless, he began to make plans for this special sibling. "She's not going to be a cheerleader, she's not wearing dresses and she's going to play baseball."

Meanwhile, Sarah's pregnancy proceeded without problems. Sarah's family and friends were going to give her a baby shower in the clubhouse at Devou Village in

Kenton Hills. Kenton Hills sits on a hillside above and adjacent to Covington, Kentucky. The panoramic views from Kenton Hills of Cincinnati are the best views of the city.

Sarah was excited to find out that expectant parents register for gifts just like couples do for their weddings. Sarah registered at a few of the big national retailers such as Target and Wal-Mart. But she also chose to sign up at a store that caters to the needs of babies.

So she registered online at Toys R Us, the national toy chain, which has a department called Babies R Us that caters to newborns and infants.

Some time later, after Sarah registered, a woman who later called herself Sarah Brody told friends she also registered at the same store.

Chapter 4

Ringing Nightmare

Another bill collector.

That's the first thought that traveled through Sarah Brady's mind when the phone rang in her house on Denver Street in Covington, Kentucky, the humble home she shared with her fiancé, Scott, and his son.

She decided to just ignore the call.

Let it ring. It's probably a telemarketer.

Besides, Sarah was busy. It was February 8, 2005, and Sarah anxiously looked forward to one of the most anticipated and important days of her life—the birth of her daughter. Since Sarah had already passed her due date, she knew that any moment labor might start and she may have to scurry off to the hospital to deliver.

Setting aside their earlier anxieties, Sarah and Scott were now planning to tie the knot after the baby arrived. Though laid off from her job as a mortgage collector for Provident Bank in Cincinnati just a few weeks earlier, Sarah, only twenty-six, made the respectable sum of $50,000 only the year before. She had never earned this much money previously. The irony that never escaped Sarah was the fact that she and Scott now faced bill collectors after she worked in collections. And that despite her early pregnancy fears she had to be philosophical about their future stability.

Sarah Brady stood just five-foot-two. She wore her naturally curly dark black hair shoulder length. She possessed a warm smile which revealed itself with ease. Sarah is an attractive young woman, with a fair complexion and easy-going manner. Thin eyebrows seemed to dance across her brow when she became animated or excited. Sarah could be described as bubbly and vibrant. When she laughed she exemplified pleasant and wholesome Midwest girl charm.

Scott poured concrete at a construction site not far away in Independence, Kentucky. Independence is a fast-growing suburb like those scattered all across the Midwest and South, a one-time farming community where subdivisions replaced tobacco fields. Concrete work is strenuous. Flat work is a method used in the concrete business. This entails pouring flat slabs of concrete for driveways and garages. This is the type of concrete Scott helped pour and finish.

Scott was not one of those boorish jocks who relive their glory days, but he still relished his accomplishments. Talking about his athletic exploits especially about his high school baseball days, invited some friendly ribbing from his family.

"My family makes a joke; they say I talk about it all the time," Scott explained.

"I'm proud of what the team and I did," Scott remarks modestly.

Pouring concrete kept Scott physically fit and kept his five-foot-ten frame lean and muscular. Shovels and special hoes are used to pour the concrete. Finishing trowels are also used to smooth concrete. Anyone working in concrete knows it's like lifting weights all day.

Sarah feels the same attraction for Scott as she did when they first started dating. He still wears his sandy blonde hair short, high and tight. Sarah and Scott's bond is obvious when they're together. Their strong feelings are conveyed as they speak and look at one another.

When Scott earned eighteen dollars an hour, he brought home a solid paycheck. Finding work at other times could be an entirely different story. Sometimes Scott only worked a few hours a week and the sporadic flow of income left Sarah frustrated. The monthly bills kept on arriving even when paychecks did not. This problem is constantly faced by millions of workers every week whose jobs are affected by inclement weather and change of season.

"Eighteen dollars an hour is great, but I would rather Scott make twelve dollars an hour and work forty hours every single week," Sarah said. "You can count on that money."

So maybe the ringing telephone was a bill collector. *Let it ring,* she told herself.

Sarah's clock in the kitchen showed 4:00 P.M., she thought of the countless errands she needed to run. Sarah planned to drive from Covington to

Independence to pick Scott up at his job site and drive back home so Scott could clean up before his son's basketball game. After the game, they were to attend a birthday party for a family member at Chuck E. Cheese, a pizza restaurant that caters to children.

Scott loved to be present at his son's basketball games. His son, though only ten years old, showed promise of becoming a fine athlete much like his father. He played for the Northern Kentucky Tarheels, one of the Cincinnati area's finest youth basketball teams. It's one of the many Amateur Athletic Union (AAU) teams which select only the best players. They play numerous games and tournaments. Having his father in the stands urging him on inspired the young boy. Scott didn't have much money to spend on his son, but he provided his son with time and support, as his own father had given him. Scott knew from his own experience of growing up without a lot of money that time and support were more essential in a father and son relationship than simply money.

Sarah didn't want to be late.

Let it ring.

But she didn't.

Unaware of how her life would forever change, she decided to answer the call. As she was about to walk out the door, Sarah almost reflexively grabbed the phone.

A woman's voice asked for Sarah.

"She's not here," Sarah answered, thinking it was either a bill collector or a telemarketer, neither of whom she wanted to deal with at the moment.

"Oh. Well, this is Sarah," the woman said. "I'll just try back."

The line went dead as the caller hung up before Sarah could respond.

Curious, Sarah glanced down at the caller ID and it read "animal shelter," but the numbers registered all zeros across the display.

"Odd," Sarah murmured to herself, "I don't know anyone at the animal shelter."

Then she remembered Scott and his brother visited the local animal shelter a week earlier looking for a dog. When Sarah and Scott met up, she told Scott about the number on the caller ID, but he couldn't shed any light as to why they would receive a call from the animal shelter.

Attending his son's basketball game and the birthday party that night, Sarah put the call out of her mind. The next morning, the phone began ringing again.

Chapter 5

Having a Baby?

A few months earlier Katie Smith announced she was going to have a baby. And she couldn't be happier.

She converted a bedroom in her small Fort Mitchell, Kentucky, apartment into a nursery complete with a crib, changing table, diapers, wipes, boxes of formula and a closet full of baby clothes.

She proudly showed off an ultrasound picture of the twins she was expecting.

She told the family that employed her as a nanny and the girls at an ice cream and sandwich shop in the tiny Ohio River city of Ludlow where she had once worked, about the pregnancy.

Already overweight, she was gaining weight, and eating more than ever and wearing maternity clothes.

She was reading novels about women with newborn babies and women who were pregnant.

Her excitement was tempered by concern, because she claimed she had previously lost two babies during delivery. Katie often lifted her shirt to show a scar across her abdomen that she claimed was the result of a Cesarean section rather than another surgery.

Yes, Katie Smith was going to have a baby. What she didn't tell anyone was she was going to have another woman's baby.

Sarah Brady's baby.

Katie Smith wasn't pregnant; despite her claims, she never had been.

All of it—the nursery, the ultrasound, the scar, the baby clothes and formula, even the maternity clothes and her bulging stomach—was part of a delusional ruse, a fake and a fraud, an escape from reality for a woman whose actual life wasn't worth living.

At age twenty-two Katie was hounded by personal demons that fueled a deep sense of insecurity and a longing to be loved and needed.

She grew up in an abusive household with a father she had accused of molesting her. She was shunned by some members of her family, a family she helped care for while growing up in Kentucky.

Overweight and unattractive, her personal appearance likely contributed to her insecurity. With a round face, large glasses with plastic frames and an often dour and defeatist attitude, she lacked the feminine charm to attract men.

Though Katie had been in short, usually troubled relationships with men, in the winter of 2004 when she was telling friends and others that she was due to have a baby in January, she was basically alone.

And while she worked in a few different jobs over the years, at a dairy bar, as a nanny and as a nurse's aid at an area hospital, Katie was at this point, unemployed and living by herself in an apartment.

In Katie's disturbed mind, a baby would change it all. It would make her happy, provide her mostly meaningless life with purpose and allow her to put behind a troubled past and look forward to a future as the mother she so badly wanted to become.

But with no man in her life, no chance at adoption, no opportunity to have that desired baby on her own, she needed a plan, a way to become a mother without ever giving birth.

So she came up with a diabolical scheme.

If she couldn't have a baby, she would kill for one.

Chapter 6

Mixed Identities

Once again the ringing phone roused Sarah from a restful sleep.

Once again she had decided she wasn't going to answer. Her baby was due very soon. Sarah was tired from the pregnancy and tired of feeling fat and uncomfortable. Even though it was close to noon she just wanted to sleep.

But the phone would not stop ringing. Scott's grandmother lived in a nursing home and called their house constantly. She worried about Sarah's pregnancy and in addition didn't have much else to do. If she didn't answer, Sarah knew Scott's grandmother would just keep calling back.

"She calls the house all day," Sarah said. "She's constantly paranoid something will go wrong with the baby. I try to be patient with her, but sometimes I'm cranky, especially when she hangs up and calls back, hangs up and calls back."

"I might as well pick it up," Sarah murmured. Still half asleep, she picked up the phone, answering the call with a drowsy "Hello."

"Sarah?" a woman's voice asked.

"I tried to reach you yesterday," the woman continued. "My name is Sarah Brody."

"That's a coincidence," Sarah said. But other than having a name that was similar to her own Sarah failed to recognize the woman's name or voice.

"I've been trying to reach you for a couple of weeks," the woman said. "I got your name from the baby registry at Toys R Us."

Sarah still sleepily mumbled, "Yeah I registered there because it's an easy method to inform some family and friends the items Scott and I desire for baby shower gifts. Anyone who buys a gift can go on the store's website, click on my name to discover what I still need or want and purchase the item by credit card."

But Sarah still wasn't sure why the woman was calling.

"Is there some problem?" Sarah slowly asked.

"I think I've got your package here."

"What package?" Sarah asked perplexed.

"The one that came in the mail," the woman said.

Sarah began to wake up but was still confused with the call.

"I have no idea what you're talking about."

"I think somebody meant to send you something through the registry and they clicked on my name by accident, because, as I found out later, my name is right below yours.

"I'm Sarah Brody and you're Sarah Brady," the

woman said. "And we live in the same state."

The woman then went into a longer explanation about how the mix-up probably occurred.

"Okay," Sarah said, "but I'm not expecting anything from anyone."

"Well, there are a few items in here," the woman said before rattling off a list of items that were in the package, including a Winnie the Pooh baby bottle.

Sarah had registered for baby items that included characters from the classic stories created by A.A. Milne. Sarah told the woman that it may indeed be her item.

Sarah asked if the package had a slip known as a gift receipt, which identifies the sender and origin of the package.

"Yeah, but my husband put it somewhere and he's out of town," she said. "I don't know where it's at."

"Are you still pregnant?" the woman asked Sarah.

At the beginning, Sarah thought nothing of being asked about her pregnancy. The woman had, after all, received baby items that were apparently intended for Sarah.

"Yes," Sarah answered.

The woman said she had contacted Toys R Us about the mix-up, but they were no help. They wouldn't take the package back.

"I would love to drop this off to you," she told Sarah. "We're in the process of moving and I'm trying to get every-thing out."

"Can I drop it off?"

Sarah was taken with the woman's offer. Since the woman went out of her way to track down the package's intended owner, Sarah didn't want to put her out.

"No," Sarah told her, "I'll just drop by your place, look at the stuff and see if it's mine. I appreciate it, but I'll come to you. There's no way I'm going to ask you to drive all the way down to Covington when you're so close to giving birth."

"Okay," the woman answered. "Can you come today?"

Sarah started thinking aloud about who could have sent the gift. "Maybe the package came from my friend, Erica, who was looking online for a certain gift. Or maybe it came from my sister, who lives in California."

"I bet it was your sister," the woman offered.

"You could be right," Sarah said.

"I'll be there early tomorrow morning," Sarah said and hung up.

Chapter 7

Strange Gifts

The northern Kentucky cities of Covington and Fort Mitchell are only a few miles apart, but worlds away from one another. Both are among the oldest communities in northern Kentucky, and since the early settlers, Covington has been a working class collection of mostly inner-city neighborhoods while Fort Mitchell has been an upscale suburb of fine homes and well-heeled residents.

Thousands of travelers pass through Covington each year, yet most don't even realize it or even bother stopping, except for gas and fast food. Interstate 75, the main route between Michigan and Florida, and all points in between, passes right through Covington, which sits at the northernmost tip of Kentucky.

Though it is Kentucky's third largest city, Covington's identity is tied to its larger neighbor to the north, Cincinnati, which sits just across from the boats going down the Ohio River. The stadiums where the Cincinnati

Reds and Cincinnati Bengals play their games, as well as Cincinnati's downtown skyline, provide stunning views from the Covington riverfront.

Covington, with about 45,000 residents, has many dimensions. Interstate 75 passes through Fort Mitchell and its suburbs. The river shoreline is lined with high rise office towers, upscale condominiums, apartments and hotels. The once thriving downtown that boasted half a dozen department stores during the post World War II boom has lost most of its vitality to the suburbs. Vacant buildings are prevalent, though some urban pioneers are staging comebacks in selected pockets being populated by bars, restaurants, wedding chapels, reception halls, some small high-tech startups and artist enclaves.

Unfortunately, Covington also has a couple of sizable housing projects that are ringed by high crime areas. But luckily through a policy of growth by annexation, it also has some modest but nice suburbs in the city's far south end, which is little more than ten miles from the Ohio River.

There are many well-kept red brick homes on one particular very quaint street in Fort Mitchell. The owners keep the lawns meticulously manicured and driveways filled with late model SUVs, minivans and sedans.

Mixed in are a few nicely maintained four-unit apartment buildings, where older couples or single men and women who have lost spouses are living out their retirements.

The apartment complex is a two-story brick with white trim, door and shutters. The living space is comprised of four units on two floors. The apartments are located atop a small hill between two neighboring single family houses on both sides. Black shingles cover the roof. The brick color of light pink brightened the appearance. The complex appeared to be built about forty years ago.

Looking around and driving slowly, Sarah soon spotted the number of the building where Sarah Brody said she lived. When Sarah Brady pulled up to the apartment house, Sarah Brody was standing in the doorway holding a cat. She was wearing pajama pants, house slippers and a gray hooded sweatshirt with pockets. "Xavier," a Catholic university in Cincinnati, was written across the front of the sweatshirt.

As Sarah pulled her SUV closer, she saw the woman in the door had a chubby face covered by a pair of round glasses and seemed very hefty or very pregnant. The woman appeared pale as if she spent a majority of her time indoors watching television or surfing the Internet.

The woman smiled when she saw Sarah pull her Cherokee SUV into the driveway and she waved, but she didn't appear very happy. Though her mouth was upturned, her face, especially her eyes, reflected an utter lack of joy. Many claim a pregnant woman glows. Staring at this woman, Sarah felt the woman standing in front of the apartment building waiting for her certainly didn't have that rosy look. The woman revealed none of the happiness associated with a "mother-to-be."

The woman held the door to the apartment building open for Sarah. They introduced themselves, walked into the building and the woman signaled that Sarah should follow her as she made an immediate right turn into her apartment. Sarah obeyed, not wanting to be rude.

Quickly, the woman shut the door behind them.

Sarah looked around. The living room was furnished with a television, love seat and chair. One side of this room contained a fireplace with a mantle. A large cardboard box, big enough for an appliance, like a refrigerator, sat in the chair. It had the same smell of your favorite aunt or grandma's apartment. The drab paint and wallpaper was probably original, Sarah observed.

For some reason, despite the furniture, the room felt empty. Then Sarah noticed there weren't any personal effects to demonstrate an imprint of who lived there. *That's strange*, Sarah thought.

"You know when you go to somebody's house and all you see is pictures," Sarah said. "Well, there was nothing like that, nothing at all."

Sarah noticed a small coffee table. Sitting on it was a laptop computer and a candle from the Yankee Candle Company, one of Sarah's favorite stores.

"Pardon me for the mess," the woman explained. "We're moving. We've got boxes everywhere."

Maybe that explains the odd feeling of the place, Sarah thought.

The woman walked into another room and came out holding a Toys R Us bag.

"I called my husband," she said. "I don't remember what he did with the air bill, but he does remember it saying 'box one of two'. I'm so sorry. I've been getting packages from everywhere."

The woman told Sarah she was from St. Louis and that she and her husband had only lived in Fort Mitchell a couple of months. They were building a house in Boone County, a neighboring county that is one of the fastest growing communities in the nation, a place where thousands of homes were gobbling up farm land and one-time tobacco fields at a rapid pace. Florence, the suburb that Scott and Sarah briefly called home, is the largest city in Boone County.

"My husband," the woman said, "is a chemical engineer." "He works for a company located just north of Cincinnati. He travels a lot," she went on.

They exchanged some more small talk before Sarah asked about the woman's baby.

"When are you due?"

"I'm overdue," the woman said. Sarah believed her based upon the woman's physical appearance.

"They are going to induce me tomorrow afternoon," she explained. "My husband is coming home tonight."

Sarah took the bag that the woman held out and looked through it. Some of the items were consistent with Sarah's registration, others were not. It was impossible to determine the sender without the gift receipt.

The woman insisted Sarah take the gifts.

"They're not mine," she said.

"It's Winnie the Pooh stuff. I'm sure it's yours."

The woman went on, "Packages from my family have been coming almost daily from St. Louis. I know for sure none of this is my stuff."

Sarah reluctantly agreed to take the bag. "I don't want to take what belongs to another expectant mother. But I'll call my sister when I get home to find out if it came from her."

"If this belongs to another woman, we need to send it to her," Sarah told the woman.

"That's fine," the woman said. "There's supposed to be another box coming. Maybe it will come to your address. Maybe it will come here. Who knows? This is kind of strange, but we'll sort it out."

The woman agreed to hang onto the gift receipt if the new package did come to her apartment.

Sarah thanked her and departed for home.

Chapter 8

Coincidence or Scheme?

A t around five o'clock Sarah called her mom and told her about the woman and the baby gifts.

"That's kind of bizarre," her mom said. "It sounds unusual to me that somebody went through all that trouble to find you."

"Maybe," Sarah murmured. "Or maybe the woman is just a good person," she paused and then went on, "Isn't it reassuring to know that there are still nice people out there?" Sarah asked her mom.

Her mom agreed but for some reason she still thought the whole thing was a little weird. Sarah's sister was at work, so Sarah decided to call that evening to find out if she had sent the packages.

When Scott came home, Sarah showed him the bag from Toys R Us.

They agreed that many of the items looked similar to those they placed on the store's registry.

"Just hang onto it and don't do anything with it until

you find out," he told her.

Later that evening, Scott was preparing to play basketball in a men's league in a neighboring town.

The phone rang and he picked it up.

"It's that woman again, the one who called earlier today," Scott stated as he handed Sarah the phone. He kissed her goodbye and walked out the door.

"I'm sorry to bother you, but I got another package and I think it's for you," the woman said almost immediately.

"Today?" Sarah asked surprised.

"Real late this afternoon," she said. "It looks like a bouncy seat. Do you want me to open it?"

"Go ahead." Sarah waited just a moment before she came back on the line.

"It is," the woman went on. "It's a Fisher Price bouncy seat."

Sarah had listed a Fisher Price bouncy seat. It couldn't be a coincidence.

"Oh gosh, this must be my stuff because there's no way the exact same one I wanted was sent to you and you didn't order it. It has to be a mistake," Sarah told her.

The woman offered to bring the package to Sarah's house.

"No, no, no, you're getting induced tomorrow afternoon," Sarah said, appreciating the offer but not wanting to impose. "Don't worry about it; I'll pick it up after you have that baby. No big deal."

The woman hesitated a moment.

"We *are* moving," the woman said. "My husband is going to have all this stuff boxed and shipped and I don't want to take it with me. I'm going to be home," she said.

Sarah took that as a hint the other woman wanted the box out of her apartment that day.

"I'll come pick it up, first thing in the morning, get it out of your way," Sarah said cheerfully. "You go have your baby and don't worry about it."

The two women appeared to be bonding. They were both young, pregnant and on the verge of giving birth to their first child. Sarah thought the woman sounded needy. By the sound of her voice and her eagerness to talk and have a visitor, Sarah discerned the woman was tired of being alone in a place where she didn't have any friends, with family out of town and a husband who traveled.

Sarah asked the woman if her husband had arrived from his business trip.

"No," the woman said, sounding a little sad. "He'll be in later tonight."

The two women talked for forty-five minutes on the phone. The woman told Sarah about her family in St. Louis, about how she thought people in the area were rude, but maybe the situation would get better when the baby was born and they were in their new house in Boone County.

Then Sarah's call waiting beeped. It was Scott on his cell phone. Sarah asked Sarah Brody to hold so she could take the call.

"Are you still on the phone with that woman?" he asked.

"She's just talking," Sarah said. "I don't want to be rude and cut her off or hang up."

"She must be really lonely," Scott said.

Sarah clicked back over to the woman after her conversa-tion with Scott. They continued to discuss babies.

Sarah knew Sarah Brody was excited about having a baby, because the woman had said she and her husband were on their third try at in-vitro fertilization.

Each time it cost $30,000—a lot of money, Sarah thought to herself.

Sarah asked the woman about adoption, but Sarah Brody explained, "There is a five year waiting list for babies in Kentucky."

"That's a really long time," Sarah said, "I've grown up around enough broken homes, poverty and teenage mothers to know there are babies that need homes."

"I keep hearing about all the babies who are abandoned," Sarah said.

"The problem," she said, "is we want a newborn. By the time parents rights are taken and given up, the baby becomes a toddler."

"That's awful," Sarah murmured.

"Besides," the woman said, "I was adopted at eight, so I really want a baby of my own."

Suddenly, the line beeped during the conversation. This time it was Scott's son's basketball coach.

"I have to take this call," Sarah finally told Sarah Brody, adding, "I'll be over to pick up the package by nine the next morning."

Not long after Sarah talked to the coach, Scott arrived home. Sarah told him about the things the woman with the baby packages had confided in her.

"She's telling you an awful lot of personal stuff,"

Scott responded.

"She must be lonely," Sarah said, feeling pity and empathy for the woman. "I'm pregnant, I know how it is. I can't imagine not having any family or any friends. It's tough not to have friends and family to support you during a difficult pregnancy. And can you imagine having a husband who travels while you're in a lonely new place?"

"Plus, she's two weeks overdue," Sarah said. "I'm feeling sorry for her. I feel badly for her."

About that time, Scott's younger brother stopped by. They told him the story about the woman, the packages, her loneliness—everything.

"I don't know," Scott's brother shook his head. "That sounds weird."

"Dude," Sarah said, "you always think everybody is weird. I'm giving her the benefit of the doubt."

"Is she friend hungry or what?" Scott's brother asked.

"I think she's very forlorn," Sarah quickly responded. "Imagine living in a place where you have no one to turn to and you're about to have your first child."

"You're just too nice," Scott's brother said to Sarah.

"Whatever," Sarah said, a little put off by his suspicions. She was just a lonely girl, a pregnant, lonely girl. She was a little clingy, but who wouldn't be in her situation?

"Maybe," Scott said. "You two can be friends."

When his brother left that day he was thinking that some-thing didn't seem right about the woman.

"I got in my truck and something told me to go back

inside," he later recalled. "I wanted to tell Sarah not to go to that woman's place. I don't know what it was, but it made me almost feel sick, like something was going to happen."

He brushed off the feelings telling himself Sarah was right, he just tended to be suspicious of strangers, and drove away.

Chapter 9

Sinister Hints

The next morning Sarah woke up at about five minutes after nine; she had planned to pick up the box of baby gifts from Sarah Brody earlier, but had overslept.

In a sleepy voice, Sarah called the other woman imme-diately. "I feel awful about being late. I know you are supposed to go for a labor inducement at a hospital in Cincinnati this afternoon," Sarah worried her mistake would disrupt the woman's schedule.

"I'm so sorry, I overslept," Sarah told her. "We can do this another time. I know you have a lot of things going on today."

"No, no," the woman insisted, "come on over, I want you to have your gift. Then I can go to the hospital with a clear head." Even Sarah thought it strange that the woman was obsessing over this trivial matter on such an important day; she told herself that all women are a little emotionally overwrought when they're about to give birth.

Once again Sarah made the short drive from her house in Covington to the woman's apartment in Fort Mitchell. The woman again waited for Sarah at the door.

Sarah said hello when she walked in and heard a strange clicking sound that immediately grabbed her attention. The woman had quickly locked the door after Sarah walked inside.

Sarah snapped her head around, looking first at the door and then the woman startled.

"Oh, I'm sorry," the woman said, obviously sensing she startled Sarah. "This door has been sticking real badly. It's a big, old wooden door and with the wood floors. They swell and stuff, and it sticks."

"I'm not locking you in," she said.

Yet, Sarah sensed uneasiness within herself.

"Where's your husband?" she asked.

The woman shook her head and sighed, "He hasn't returned from his business trip."

Sarah couldn't believe it. The woman was getting induced that day. She was going to have a baby, and her husband wasn't going to be there.

"You're getting induced today," Sarah blurted out, "what do you mean he's not home?"

"He called me late last night and said he got stuck," the woman said wistfully. "He'll be here later in the morning."

Something about the scene made her uneasy. Despite just arriving, Sarah wanted to pick up her package and leave.

"Well, we better hurry up since you've got to go to the hospital," Sarah encouraged.

"Let me get your stuff," Sarah Brody responded.

The woman walked into another room and returned a moment later with a baby seat. Sarah relaxed a little, it was the same one that Sarah had placed on her Toys R Us registry.

"Yeah, that's mine," Sarah said, "I'm still curious about who sent it.

"Do you have the gift receipt?" Sarah asked.

The woman glanced around the apartment. "Now where did I put that?" she asked herself out loud.

For about fifteen minutes the woman searched for the gift receipt without success.

"You're pregnant and you just forget things," she explained.

The uneasy feeling returned. Sarah wanted so badly to leave; she faked small talk but was getting more restless.

"Yeah, you do forget a lot of things. You're so tired and worn out when you're pregnant," Sarah agreed. "You know what, it's no big deal. After you have the baby we'll figure it out. I need to call my sister anyway and find out if she sent it."

"No, no, no," Sarah Brody insisted. "Let me find it, let me find the damn thing."

The woman continued scampering out and picking things up and putting them down as she strode through the apartment. Sarah followed her through the living room, around a corner into a dining room, past the kitchen into a bedroom. Then they circled back through into the dining room where a high chair had been set up.

"That's cute," Sarah commented.

"I got that for twenty dollars at Target," the woman said, sounding proud for picking up what she characterized as a bargain. "It was on clearance."

Again, Sarah was feeling a little sorry for the woman. She looked preoccupied and worried and was very needy of attention. No wonder, Sarah thought, she was scheduled to have a baby *that* day and her husband wasn't around; she had no family in town and it seemed like the only friend she had was Sarah, who barely knew her.

Then Sarah Brody led her into the next room—a fully equipped nursery. "Isn't it wonderful?" she asked, not waiting for an answer.

Clearly, the woman seemed excited to be pregnant. She was eager to talk about her pregnancy, anxious to share stories with another pregnant woman and proud to show off how she was preparing for motherhood.

And the room showed care and good taste. Sarah Brody had everything prepared: a crib equipped with full bedding, a changing table, diapers, wipes, and a child's twin bed covered by a comforter of a nighttime scene filled with moons and stars.

On the floor sat boxes stacked full of baby clothes and free samples of formula which expectant mothers receive. Sarah Brody opened a closet and the contents stunned Sarah.

It bulged with clothes and baby items. "We're talking full out," Sarah would later recall.

"Look at all this stuff," the woman said, showing off a little. "My family keeps sending me more things for the baby. I'm so lucky."

They walked out of the nursery, down a short

hallway back into the living room and then into the woman's bedroom.

"Maybe I left the gift receipt in here somewhere," the woman said.

As the woman rummaged through her dresser, Sarah just stood there, glancing around feeling a little uncomfortable. The room was pink and lacy. It didn't look like a room a couple shared; it looked like a woman's bedroom.

"It was," Sarah would later say, "girlie."

One closet the woman opened in the bedroom had plenty of women's clothes, but Sarah immediately noticed there were no men's clothes at all.

Turning, Sarah noticed a pack of cigarettes and a picture of a woman. It sat on a nightstand. This would be the only picture Sarah saw in the house. Sarah asked about the picture. Sarah Brody simply said it was a friend.

Sarah continued to glance around the room. She looked over toward the dresser and spotted something very strange, even bizarre.

There, on the dresser, was a picture cut out of a magazine of the four women from *Sex and the City*, the popular HBO cable television show starring Sarah Jessica Parker. *Sex and the City* is the comedy about women, dating, relationships and friendships in New York City. It had won numerous Emmy's and was not only funny, but racy. Nudity and graphic language on the show was common. After several tremendously successful seasons, it was now off the air.

However, it was what had been done to the picture that made Sarah stare at it.

The faces of the four leading ladies on the show were scratched out and someone had written names above them. Sarah could decipher only one name— Sarah Fay.

What the hell is that? Sarah thought to herself.

At that moment Sarah Brody then turned to Sarah.

"I think I put the receipt in a box under my bed; I think that's what I did with it."

Sarah Brody rubbed her hands across her bulging belly and then nodded her head toward the bed. She smiled. "I don't think I can get down there."

"I will," Sarah said without hesitation, bending down to look under the bed.

"There's nothing here," she called out.

"Oh, okay, I just don't know what I did with it," Sarah Brody shook her head, "I'll to go back to the living room to check the drawer in my television stand."

The woman moved out of the room. "Come on," she called to Sarah. Sarah stood up from her crouched position next to the bed. "I'll be right there." As she rose she looked at the nightstand and saw an inhaler, the kind for people with asthma or breathing problems. Without thinking she picked it up and recoiled in shock.

There was a name on it. It wasn't Sarah Brody.

The name was Katie Smith.

What in the world did it mean? Had Sarah picked up someone's inhaler by mistake? Had someone been visiting and left it here? Or was it something more ominous?

Chapter 10

Fear

Sweeping chills rushed over Sarah. Her prior uncomfortable feelings turned to fear. Her heart began to race. Her palms began sweating. She felt perspiration on her forehead. Her thoughts quickened as their meeting flashed through her mind. Disturbing visions swirled in her head.

The phone calls out of the blue.

The woman's insistence on getting close to Sarah.

The fact that this woman said she was scheduled to have a baby that day and her husband wasn't there.

In fact, as her mind now saw it, there was no sign that a husband was ever around.

The pack of cigarettes on the nightstand.

For a woman so concerned about her pregnancy and her baby, why was she smoking?

Now Sarah began to put some of the disparate pieces together. The lost shipping receipt was starting to sound like a story; perhaps the receipt never existed.

Who was this woman? Why was she now in Sarah's life? What was she up to?

As more and more thoughts raced through Sarah's mind, she became aware that during the entire time she had been in the apartment she never put down her car keys. Perhaps it was her gut instilling fear. She wasn't about to put them down now. As long as she kept the keys in her hand, Sarah believed if anything bad happened she could take off and get away in her car. At any rate, she could breathe easier and she now felt prepared.

Slowly, Sarah walked back into the living room. The woman, Sarah Brody, Katie Smith, or whoever she was, was now rifling through papers on the television stand drawer, periodically stopping to look at her cell phone. As Sarah watched the woman more closely, she stepped over to the phone in the apartment and picked it up while simultaneously explaining, "I'm calling my husband."

The woman's voice rose, "You better get home or you better call me back." The woman left a message in an annoyed voice for her husband.

The uncomfortable situation grew more uneasy as the woman turned to Sarah, "I'm afraid he may be having an extramarital affair with another woman." Sarah took a deep breath not knowing how to respond.

"I think he's cheating on me. I think that's where he is right now. He probably spent the night with his girlfriend." The woman went on, becoming visibly agitated.

"That's terrible," Sarah said feeling more and more uncomfortable. The woman continued to talk, becoming more and more personal and filling Sarah with a growing feeling of dread.

Sarah tried to reassure her, "I'm sure he's not cheating on you. Lot's of women are nervous about that when they're pregnant."

"He's cheated on me before," the woman responded. "He didn't want to try for this baby. But the reason I got the third in-vitro was because I caught him cheating and told him either we have another in vitro or I'm leaving."

As the woman grew more agitated, Sarah became more nervous. Sarah tried to calm her down to the best of her abilities.

"I'm sure he's still at work," Sarah offered as an explanation.

"I don't know," the woman said as the anger grew in her voice. "Let me go see if I can find that paper. You need to know who sent you your stuff and I'm so distracted with my problems. I just don't know what I did with it."

The paper again! This search had gone on for far too long. Sarah just wanted to leave. She wanted to forget about the damn receipt and go home.

The woman strode back into the bedroom. Sarah, now alone in the living room, already unnerved and leery, heard a scream that punctured the uncomfortable silence.

Sarah's whole body jumped. Every nerve tingled. "What the hell's that?" Sarah cried aloud as she rushed into the bedroom, the screams continuing and growing louder.

"Sarah!" the woman screamed.

Sarah reached the bedroom. The woman lay sprawled on the floor.

"I think I'm in labor!" she screamed. "Can you help me get to the bathroom?"

Sarah bent over to try to pick the woman up and began walking backwards into the bathroom. Every muscle in Sarah's body strained with the effort. Suddenly Sarah's grasp of the woman's arm and shoulder began to slip. Worried about taking on this task when she herself was eight and a half months pregnant, Sarah could not believe she now had to carry the woman. But she could think of nothing else to do, she couldn't leave the woman lying there. The woman literally hung on Sarah's arms as they reached the small and cramped bathroom. Quickly scanning the room, Sarah saw the bathroom had a dual tub and bath. A toilet and sink barely fit on the other side of the bathroom. The floor was covered with cheap linoleum. No pictures hung on the wall.

As the woman cried, Sarah tried to maneuver her into the bathroom, but the space was too cramped. Two women, each nine months pregnant, could not squeeze into the tiny room.

At that moment and to Sarah's utmost shock, the woman stared directly into Sarah's eyes. In that short time frame it was as if "Sarah Brody" instantly transformed from a frantic mother on the verge of giving birth to someone fanatic and suddenly composed, but frightening.

Sarah began to shiver as she watched the evilness pour out of the woman's face. Sarah trembled all over. Sarah released her grip on the woman; she felt paralyzed by it. The woman blocked Sarah's exit through the bathroom door. At this point, Sarah was in the bathroom and the woman by the door. Sarah took a deep breath.

Trying to calm the situation, Sarah asked the woman to check and see if her water had actually broken.

When the woman moved, Sarah seized the opportunity to brush by her, make her way from the bathroom and back down the hallway toward the front door of the apartment. Sarah couldn't stop shaking as she stepped into the living room, and grabbed her purse that she set down earlier.

"I've got to get out of here as fast as possible," Sarah mumbled to herself. As Sarah made this decision, the woman came out of the bathroom and, surprisingly, lit up a cigarette, acting as if nothing had happened the last several minutes. The woman's demeanor had completely changed.

"I don't know what's wrong," the woman said, a little too calmly and matter-of-factly for Sarah.

"You need to call the doctor or 911," Sarah told her urgency in her voice. "Your husband isn't here and I don't know what to do if you start to go into labor."

"Just please stay and talk to me until after I talk to the doctor," the woman begged.

"I'll call the doctor right now. Just please don't go."

The woman then asked Sarah another odd question.

"How do you know if your water breaks?"

"You will know if your water breaks!" Sarah responded with fear and trepidation giving away to, at least momentarily, irritation with the woman's ignorance.

"I don't know," the woman said. "It's my first kid." She looked away as if not wanting to engage.

The woman picked up the phone and left Sarah to walk into the kitchen. Sarah overheard her message to the doctor. She actually gave her name and address over the phone.

"That's funny," Sarah murmured.

Sarah found contents of the message unusual—who calls their doctor and says their name and address like that? Name, sure. Address, never.

The woman returned to the living room after making the short call to the doctor.

"He told me I'll be fine once I'm induced and I'm okay as long as I don't start having contractions. Do you think you can stay with me until my husband gets here?"

"I don't think I can."

Sarah made up her mind—she wasn't staying. There was something more here, something making her very afraid.

"You have to call 911. They'll send an ambulance if your water breaks and labor starts."

"I've got to go. I've got to pick up my stepson. He has a doctor's appointment."

The woman snapped back at Sarah.

"Where's his mom?" the woman said, raising her voice to a near shout mixed with ambivalence.

Sarah explained, "The boy's mom, stepdad and dad are all at work. I'm the only one available to take him to the appointment."

"I really do have to go right now. And the doctor said you'll be okay," Sarah cajoled.

The woman hesitated, as if about to protest. Clearly she did not want Sarah to leave.

"Do you have to?"

"I really do."

"Let me get you those formula coupons." The woman ran back to the bedroom.

But Sarah felt a sense of urgency; she didn't want to be here with this strange woman any longer.

"Come on," Sarah murmured, prodding herself. I've got to get out of here. I'm not falling for any more of this woman's histrionics and stories. There's something ominous about her.

The woman came back in the room and handed over the coupons. Sarah nervously and casually flipped through them. Suddenly, she stumbled upon one where she stopped. Her heart began to beat frantically.

This coupon was labeled, "Especially for Katie Smith."

Chapter 11

Death Match

At that point, Sarah didn't know who the woman standing in front of her was. Maybe it was Katie Smith, the name that showed up first on the inhaler and now on the baby coupons. Maybe it wasn't. Sarah was now convinced though, it certainly wasn't someone named Sarah Brody.

"Well," Sarah said, growing more unsettled and scared with each passing moment, "I better go. I have to be there at eleven and it's probably about 10:30."

Sarah threw her purse strap over her shoulder which is a woman's common signal she is ready to leave. It's the same as standing up at the end of a meeting. The message is—it's time to go.

"You've been so nice," the woman said. "Can I give you a hug?"

A hug? Hugging this woman was the last thing Sarah wanted to do. She wanted to leave, not embrace this strange woman. Sarah didn't need a hug from her.

Sarah tried to spurn her with body language by standing near the apartment's front door with her arms at her side and her hands clasping her purse and keys. The two women stood face to face.

Insistent, the woman reached out and grabbed Sarah with an unwarranted and unilateral hug. She squeezed Sarah tight, too tight for a friendly embrace. As the woman hugged her, Sarah began to pull back. At that moment, Sarah's horrific nightmare began. As Sarah backed away, the woman reached in the front pocket of her sweatshirt and pulled out a knife whose sharp blade glittered in the light.

"Bitch," the woman screamed in a voice that terrified Sarah, "you're not going anywhere."

What was the woman talking about? Sarah froze, confused.

Until that quivering moment, Sarah Brady had lived what most would consider a life of hardships, trials and tribulations. The elements of those years now flashed before her.

She saw herself when she held titles as honor student, cheerleader and homecoming queen in school. Then she recalled how sad she'd been when it came time for college, lack of money thwarted that option and Sarah never was able to save enough to go and she was afraid of taking on loans she couldn't pay.

Her memories brought visions of Scott. She loved the father of her child, but the two had not married. He dropped out of college. Never marrying yet calling someone your fiancé for years and years felt awkward. It always sounds fabricated to others. Sarah earned decent money working in collections at a bank, but after being laid off by February of 2005, she was unemployed.

So Sarah saw her life; it was not charmed, privileged or enviable. But there is an old adage which is this: You don't learn anything from the easy stuff in life; it's the tough times that teach lessons, forge character, create a sense of appreciation, establish character and make you what is called a survivor.

Not a survivor on a reality television show.

A survivor of the grim reality of life.

Maybe, as Sarah Brody, Katie Smith or whatever her name, lifted that knife over her head, all that Sarah learned over the years kicked in and took over.

Whatever it was that prepared her as the woman moved to thrust a knife in her, Sarah felt two distinct emotions. She felt a deep love for the child she carried in her womb and the courage to fight to the death to save herself and her unborn child.

Sarah had no idea why this woman, pregnant herself, was threatening her and her unborn child. But Sarah sure as hell wasn't going to allow the strange female to kill Sarah or her baby.

"I guess," Sarah said later, "that my maternal instincts just took over."

Roughly the same height, the two women stood toe to toe, face to face. They were both in their ninth month of pregnancy about to engage in a real life death match, but why? Sarah had no clue, but she was ready to defend herself and her baby.

Warmth flooded over her. Maybe it was adrenaline; maybe it was fear. She took her left hand and knocked the knife out of the woman's hand.

The battle continued. The woman spun around, grabbed Sarah's hair which was styled in a short ponytail, and yanked it forcefully. At the same time the woman moved forward, flipping Sarah over the arm of the dusty love seat.

A second later, the woman landed on top of Sarah and started whaling, punching her in the head, shoulders and arms. Mustering up her remaining strength, Sarah managed to fend off some of the punches and rolled over on top of the woman. Then she jumped up from the love seat and ran toward the door.

Sarah managed to unlock the front door, but she lost track of her purse and keys. "Never mind," she whispered to herself, "No time to stop. I'll leave them behind."

The main front door of the apartment building remained open. A screen door is all that stood between Sarah and freedom from this violent nightmare. But could she get out? Sarah tried to flip the door handle to open it, but the woman grabbed Sarah's shirt and stretch pants pulling her back into the apartment.

Sarah's heart pounded like the hooves of a horse sprinting down the home stretch. Light streamed into the dreary and dusky apartment from the screen door. As Sarah grasped the door handle, she felt like the girl running in the horror movies who is inevitably caught and dies a horrible death at the hands of a serial killer.

Then, as if from deep within her, Sarah began screaming, "Oh my God, help me, help me, help me!!"

As if in response, the woman released her clutch on Sarah's clothes, but then her face filled with fury and she caught a full hand of Sarah's hair. With her other hand she tried to cover Sarah's mouth.

"You stupid bitch," the woman said with an icy calmness. "No one can hear you. Quit screaming."

The woman pulled Sarah's head back. Sarah kicked and screamed, trying to stay in the hallway. Didn't anyone hear her? Was anyone at home in the other apartments? Maybe that's why the woman decided to strike during the middle of the day, when the other tenants were at work or someplace else.

Sarah's head snapped back in a whiplash fashion. As Sarah whipped around, she again found herself face to face with the woman. Once again, Sarah sensed the aura of a demon. As Sarah screamed, the woman used one of her hands to suppress the shrill sound by covering Sarah's mouth. "God help me now. I haven't any more strength," Sarah cried softly.

The woman gripped Sarah's hair tighter and literally dragged her backwards. Sarah's feet slid across the slick well worn wooden floor back through the doorway. Sarah cried uncontrollably.

It was at that moment when Sarah thought for the first time that she might not survive that a vision came to her.

Images of Scott and his son flashed before her eyes.

Now, as the beating and the pain intensified, Sarah thought there was a real possibility she would die on the floor of the stranger's apartment.

But why? Why would this woman want Sarah's child? Who was she? Why was she trying to beat Sarah to death? The woman tried to shut the door. She was very strong and weighed over two hundred pounds. She used her strength and weight to drag Sarah back into the apartment.

As the woman pushed Sarah to the ground, Sarah's face hit the floor. Pain shot through her entire body. The pressure of the woman's weight pressed against Sarah's unborn baby.

Sarah found herself face down with the woman on top of her back. The woman grabbed a heavy clear glass dish—an ash tray or maybe a candy dish—and began using it to pummel the back of Sarah's head.

Suddenly something clicked inside of Sarah Brady. She had come too far from the trailer parks, the cramped apartments, the pitiful Christmas mornings and the desperation of a life growing up in poverty to allow this woman to snuff out her life.

Even though she grew up in some tough neighborhoods, Sarah had never been a fighter. She can only remember being in one physical fight in her life, and that was a minor altercation in high school when she stood up to a female bully. Yet, she found the strength, the kind that comes from God and infuses the heart and manifests in the muscles, to try to throw the woman off her back and climb on top of her.

Now, Sarah decided, it was her turn. She grabbed the dish away from her attacker and began striking the woman as hard as she could. Many of the blows landed directly on the woman's already battered head. At first the woman resisted. Then she lay still.

A moment earlier Sarah thought she was going to die; now though, she was concerned about taking this woman's life. However, she knew she had to do something and quickly before the woman came to and began to attack her again.

Sarah threw the dish across the room. She jumped off the woman, grabbed her own purse and car keys and once again headed for the door. She didn't have nearly as much time to escape as she had anticipated.

Somehow the woman stood up. But how? Sarah had just beaten the woman with a heavy glass dish for what seemed like five minutes. Sarah was hysterical, bent over, breathing hard and grabbing her stomach in pain.

The woman just stood there, icy calm as if nothing had happened.

"You're not going anywhere," the woman spat out at Sarah.

Sarah was numb for a moment then she began to slowly creep toward the door. But the woman moved toward Sarah.

"Just shut up," the woman said, once again with a voice so calm and collected that it resonated pure evil. "I wasn't going to hurt you. But you said you were going to leave, and everybody leaves me."

"How can she be so calm after the beating she gave me?" Sarah thought.

Tears running down her face, Sarah talked about her baby, talked about the woman and *her* baby.

"We have to go to the hospital!" Sarah screamed through the tears. "What about your baby?"

"I'm not going to the hospital. And neither are you. Just sit on the couch and listen to what I have to say."

"No," Sarah insisted. "I'm leaving."

"No you're not," the woman responded.

The woman ignored Sarah's pleas. Even begging for medical attention for their unborn children failed to move the woman. The woman brushed her hand across

Sarah's face and said in a guttural tone, "You have to stay here. I won't let you go." Strangely, in the middle of this violent altercation, she mentioned her husband would be arriving home soon and they needed to clean up the mess. Sarah couldn't believe it. Meanwhile, Sarah's body heaved fighting for air, exhausted. Tears wet her blouse. She realized reason would not convince this irrational woman to stop. The woman repeated, "Under no condition will I allow you to leave." Sarah scanned the room with puffy and swollen eyes. Searching for a way to get away, she saw no opening. The woman retreated for a moment. Sarah cried harder, "Let me go!"

Sarah began moving toward the front door. For the first time, she called the woman by the name she had seen on the inhaler and the coupons—Katie. Perhaps that would make her leave Sarah alone.

It had the opposite effect. As soon as Sarah spoke the name "Katie," the woman charged at her with the knife in her hand. The use of the word "Katie" clearly sparked fury in the woman. Sarah believed this disclosure shattered the fairy tale world of her attacker.

Maybe while they were on the floor fighting, the woman found the knife. That's probably why she wasn't resisting Sarah's beating. She managed to get a hand on the knife and hid it under her body.

Now, she came quickly at Sarah, lunging with the knife near Sarah's belly, "I want that baby." Sarah made a snap decision. She grabbed the blade of the knife with her bare and unprotected hand as the woman came toward her. The women slammed into a wall, but Sarah still held onto the knife blade even as it painfully sliced a cut into her hand.

Unable to swing or plunge the knife because of Sarah's grip, the woman started to use her body as a weapon, slamming into Sarah and pinning her against the fireplace mantle. She hit Sarah like a football player hits a blocking dummy.

The woman struggled to free the knife from Sarah's grip. With her other hand, she grabbed Sarah's head and repeatedly slammed it into the brick of the fireplace. The pain in Sarah's hand from the knife was excruciating. But Sarah would not release the knife, even though the knife continued its damage to her hand. Sarah tightened her grip believing releasing the knife meant certain death.

The women collided into the coffee table where a portable telephone was perched. With the knife still in one hand, Sarah swooped down grabbing the phone. She tried to call 911. She dialed the number and screamed, "Help!" but had no way of knowing whether or not it connected, because she never put the phone to her ear.

Still locked in battle, each woman had one arm raised as they fought for the knife. Their other arms hung down below their waists as they struggled for the phone.

As the woman desperately tried to grab the phone out of Sarah's hand, the woman loosened her grip on the knife. Sarah felt the release of tension. Seizing the opportunity, Sarah twisted the knife and then grasped it.

Sarah grasped the knife in her left hand.

The women broke apart. Once again Sarah began

moving toward the door, brandishing the weapon. She hoped against hope that might deter her attacker, but the woman came at her despite Sarah's grip on the knife. Sarah began wildly swinging the weapon, a four-inch hunting knife with a four-inch black handle.

The woman blocked Sarah's exit through the door, but Sarah continued to swing the knife and moved away from the fireplace mantle and toward the door.

The woman moved toward her. Sarah swung again. This time, the knife blade struck the woman and Sarah felt the difference from the previous swings.

Sarah had stabbed the woman in the shoulder.

The woman fell back into the love seat in the living room in stunned silence. As she began to cry, she pulled a bloody hand away from her wounded shoulder.

Sarah froze. "Oh my God," she murmured, "I just stabbed a pregnant woman. But I had no choice," she told herself. "I had to save my baby."

Even though the woman seemed numbed, Sarah didn't know if or when she would attack Sarah again. Desperate, Sarah knew she had better flee the apartment and find help. As Sarah tried to escape, the woman quickly stood up and lunged at her yet again. Sarah couldn't believe it.

"You stupid bitch, you fucking stabbed me!" she screamed at Sarah as she charged.

The women once again began to struggle. This time Sarah had the advantage. She shoved the woman, throwing her up against the love seat. The woman bounced off the furniture and hit her head against the wall.

Slumped against the wall, bloodied from the beating

and the stabbing, the woman just looked up at Sarah without a word, her eyes staring up without seeing.

Sarah, with the phone in one hand and the knife in the other, turned and ran out of the apartment as fast as a nine-month pregnant woman could run.

Chapter 12

Run For Your Life

Fleeing the apartment, Sarah was hysterical and disheveled —a scary sight for anyone in what was usually a quiet neighborhood: a nine-month pregnant woman, running into the February cold with no coat, carrying a bloody knife in her hand, screaming as she ran down the concrete steps to the street below.

It was a very cold and clear February morning, like so many other winter days in the Midwest. Though it had snowed a lot that winter, no snow blanketed the ground.

In her frenzy to run away from the woman's apartment, Sarah left her keys and purse. It was useless to run to her car. Instead, she headed to the street, hoping to flag someone down and obtain help. She tried to calm herself but was frightened and weeping uncontrollably. Sarah was panicking. How badly was she cut? Was her baby okay? What about the woman she left behind? The two had fought ferociously. How badly was the woman injured and was her baby in danger?

A red Jeep Cherokee driven by an elderly woman drove down the road. As Sarah approached the street, the driver stopped. However, seeing the sight of a bloody, knife-toting pregnant woman screaming hysterically while running into the street made her fearful of stopping to help.

Instead, the woman continued to drive. Sarah began babbling and shrieking, trying to tell the gray-haired woman about the horror that had just occurred in the apartment.

"I need help!" Sarah screamed. "Call the police! Call 911! A woman just tried to kill me!"

The woman recoiled.

"There's a police station down the street," the woman said before rolling up her window and driving away.

Unbelievable, Sarah thought. *Won't anyone help me?* She stared up and down the quiet solitude of the suburban street. No one was outside on this cold day. She saw no lights or movement. From all appearances, it looked as if no one was home at most of the houses. She had to do something and quickly.

Even though she was nine months pregnant, Sarah began running uphill toward Dixie Highway, the main north-south thoroughfare through Fort Mitchell and much of Kenton County.

The woman said there is a police station on Dixie Highway. Sarah decided she had no choice but to find it.

Exhausted and out of breath, Sarah struggled running the hundred or so yards to the corner of Dixie.

At the heavily-traveled intersection, she stumbled partially out into the street and began frantically waving her arms.

Almost immediately, a minivan pulled around the corner. A dark haired woman who looked to be in her thirties was at the wheel of the vehicle. A young girl, presumably the woman's daughter, was also inside the van.

Sarah was afraid the woman would be as apprehensive as the elderly driver. "She probably had been wondering what on earth was going on," Sarah said later. "My hair was matted and flying in the wind, I had a phone in one hand, the knife in the other. I was bleeding, I looked pretty banged up, pretty scary."

The van stopped and a woman got out and checked on Sarah, trying to calm her down. Sarah couldn't stand it any longer. Physically and mentally exhausted, bleeding from her wounds and terrified about what just happened, she fell to the ground, sobbing, on a small and grassy median.

Unlike the previous driver, the woman from the van never hesitated as she approached Sarah. Sarah gazed at the woman, then at the young girl who was probably nine or ten and dropped the knife and the phone she had been clutching since fleeing the apartment moments earlier.

The little girl staring at Sarah broke into tears.

"To this day I don't know who the lady was," Sarah later said of her Good Samaritan. "But I know how much I scared her little girl. I looked horrible. I had blood all over me, I was crying. It was bad." I blurted out, "I've been attacked; she wanted my baby!"

But none of that stopped the woman from calling 911 as soon as she got to her nearby home.

Seemingly, seconds later, a police cruiser pulled up. Help at last. Sarah began to feel some sense of relief for the first time since the entire ordeal.

Fort Mitchell Police Chief Steve Hensley was a veteran officer known for his professionalism, compassion, easy-going manner and ability to deal with the public he served. About five ten and attractive in his forties, his hair had begun to gray a little. He wore a mustache on an otherwise clean-cut face.

Chief Hensley had risen through the ranks at the small suburban police department, starting at the bottom of the rung as a patrolman. His management and organizational skills were impressive enough that just five months after Sarah Brady was attacked, the City Council of Fort Mitchell elevated Hensley to city administrator while allowing him to remain Chief of Police as well. It's a high honor for him in a city that has always been efficiently operated. Chief Hensley led his department of officers. One of his officers, Specialist Scott Nealy, was the officer who arrived on the scene.

Nealy dashed out of his car and helped Sarah to her feet.

"What's wrong? Do you have any weapons?" Nealy asked, doing his job as a police officer as he offered aide while also patting Sarah down so he could determine if she was concealing a knife, gun or other weapon.

"No," Sarah said suddenly becoming aware of what Nealy was looking for.

"It's in the grass," she said, referring to the knife.

Nealy helped Sarah to his cruiser and set her partially in the backseat. She sat down with her legs still outside the car.

"Are you hurt?" Nealy asked.

Sarah really wasn't sure. She knew she had been cut, but didn't know if she had actually been stabbed. At the moment she felt numb; she didn't feel pain or emotion.

"I don't know," she replied.

Noting Sarah's labored breathing, faltering vital signs and condition, the officers radioed for an ambulance. Soon it arrived. The medics transferred Sarah from the cruiser to the ambulance. Emergency technicians immediately took off her shirt to check her and the baby for wounds or problems.

Specialist Nealy tried his best to keep Sarah calm. But when the emergency medical technicians said they were leaving for the hospital, Nealy said, "You can't go anywhere."

Nealy wanted to preserve any potential crime scene; he also intended to question Sarah about what happened. Investigators believe it is imperative to interrogate participants or witnesses involved in crimes as soon as possible after an incident has occurred. Even after a few moments, details and memories blur, so police prefer to obtain the facts while they are still fresh in someone's mind.

"Oh yeah," the man in the ambulance told Nealy. "We're leaving, we're leaving. Her heartbeat is erratic."

Oh my God, Sarah thought. She felt her heart pounding. The ambulance crew seemed more worried about Sarah than the baby.

"Are you okay?" they kept asking her. "Just tell us

what happened."

"She came after me and I stabbed her," Sarah blurted out. "She's bleeding. I stabbed her somewhere in the shoulder. I saw it. She's bleeding."

The admission from Sarah gave Nealy a renewed sense of urgency. He continued to press his case. His backup had not yet arrived, so Nealy could not run to the apartment to check on the woman who Sarah wounded until another officer arrived. "Look," the man in the ambulance told Nealy. "I'm leaving. This lady is going to go into cardiac arrest. You know where I'll be, Saint E's."

With that, the medic shut the door and the ambulance sped off toward the hospital.

Chapter 13

Scene of the Crime

Specialist Scott Nealy arrived first at Katie Smith's apartment and rushed inside. Very soon after, Sergeant Bussman responded to the 911 call along with Specialist Taylor and headed for Katie Smith's address.

While Nealy attempted to asses the situation, Sergeant Bussman and Officer Taylor entered the apartment and located Katie Smith in the living room lying on her back. Katie was breathing but unresponsive. She had a visible bloodstain near her left breast and was gasping for air. The living room was in disarray. Two bloodstains were visible on the white fireplace mantle. Several cigarette butts were scattered on the floor. The couch was pushed over and the coffee table was on its side in the living room. Parts of a broken candleholder were lying in the floor and a pool of a red substance was near the end table. The police later determined the substance to be candle wax. The officers searched the rest of the apartment to check for other injured parties and did not find anyone besides Katie.

Specialist Best showed up at the scene and secured the perimeter of Katie Smith's apartment with crime tape and maintained the perimeter pending a search warrant. Bill Crockett and Terry Williams of the Kenton County Commonwealth Attorney's Office arrived to assess the scene.

Both Crockett and Williams accompanied Sergeant Bussman to the Fort Mitchell Police Department and assisted in creating an application and affidavit in support of a search warrant.

Immediately, Sergeant Bussman drove to the residence of Judge Marty Sheehan of the Kenton County District Court and obtained a search warrant for Katie Smith's apartment.

Afterward, Bussman drove back to Smith's apartment and met up with members of the Fort Mitchell Crime Scene team. Specialists Taylor, Best, Zerhusen and Berwanger executed the search warrant. Crime Scene Team members photographed, collected, and processed evidence.

Meanwhile, Specialist Taylor responded to the complaint at Katie Smith's apartment where the stabbing took place. Upon arrival, he observed that the door to the first floor apartment was not closed, but standing slightly ajar. After knocking and not receiving a response, Sergeant Bussman and Officer Taylor stated, "Police!" and entered the apartment. Upon entry they observed Katie lying on her back wearing a blood stained sweatshirt and panties. Katie was moaning and being unresponsive. He notified dispatch that they needed paramedics to immediately respond to the apartment. Specialist Taylor continued trying to get Katie to respond, but was unsuccessful in his efforts. Katie then rolled onto her right side and remained in this position until squad personnel rolled her onto her back. They cut her sweatshirt finding the puncture wound in her left chest area. The Emergency Medical Services arrived providing medical care for several minutes.

The Fort Mitchell Life Squad members who came to the scene to care for Katie were Brian Kinsley, Adam Fuller, Jay Kelley and John Herman. Barb Bell and Loraine Traylor were the transcare EMTs who also arrived at the scene. Specialists Tim Berwanger, Bill Zerhusen and Matt Robinson took photographs to document the crime. Detective Terry Williams from the Commonwealth Attorney's office accompanied Bill Crockett at the scene as well.

Emergency Medical Services personnel entering the apartment began treating Katie. They brought her into the ambulance and transported her to the hospital. Meeting with Specialist Nealy, Specialist Taylor contained the scene on Sergeant Bussman's instruction. The EMS intended to transport Sarah Brady to the hospital. Specialist Nealy showed Sergeant Bussman the knife and a telephone that was lying on the sidewalk. Specialist Nealy followed the life squad to the hospital and Officer Bussman kept the phone and knife until Detective Nottingham arrived and took custody of the evidence.

Meanwhile, police officers took extensive photographs of the crime scene and logged them in.

The photos reflected an obvious struggle between

two people inside the apartment. Blood was splattered and smeared everywhere. Items were broken. They also revealed a "belly suit" and countless baby related items. At this point in time the police had every reason to believe a crime took place. But why? The wounds inflicted on Katie included one on the upper left chest, lower back on the left side, left tricep, right upper shoulder and on the hands.

Later, Sarah accurately described the clothing located in the closet as the same items Katie had been wearing at the time of the attack. A sweatshirt stuffed with the same type of padding was also located by the police.

The apartment reflected an impending birth. Katie had a fully stocked nursery with everything a new mother needed for a newborn. However, it also reflected a strange atmosphere. A zippered pouch was located in Katie's living room. It contained surgical gloves, hemostats, surgical scissors, gauze and a clip designed for closing the plastic inserts on a baby bottle. Later, the police surmised the intended use of the clip was to cut the umbilical cord. There were medical absorbent pads in Katie's bedroom.

As they investigated, the police discovered Katie Smith registered herself as pregnant with a listed January 6, 2005 due date on the Toys R Us/Babies R Us Expectant Mothers Registry. She had most likely checked the registry and discovered a 'Sarah Brady' with a Covington address. And in the end Katie chose a name with only a one letter difference. In Katie's home, the police found Sarah Brady's name, phone number and address written in crayon on a piece of paper. Obviously Katie considered stealing other identities. Another name was also written on the paper. The second woman listed a due date of February 3, 2005 and the first woman listed a due date of February 1, 2005, and had her baby on January 17, 2005 and was unlisted in the phone book. Sarah Brady was listed in the phone book. There was even a third woman who was a possibility. But her due date was listed as March 30, 2004. The second woman was saved by an earlier due date. The third woman was saved by a later due date. Unfortunately, Sarah Brady was not as lucky.

The police discovered more possible evidence that Katie had fastened on Sarah Brady as the person who could satisfy her yearning desire for a baby. Had a diabolical plan been forming in her mind to confuse the identity of the two women? Had she activated her plan when a package arrived at her home addressed to Sarah Brady of Covington?

Whether Katie had sent herself the package creating the opportunity or just seized it was unknown. However, the police felt that Katie may have surmised she was out of time and had to either kidnap a baby or create yet another tale of tragedy to explain the baby's absence. They felt Katie could have used either the internet or telephone book to find Sarah Brady's phone number, confirmed that the information regarding her expected delivery was correct and lured Sarah to her home. Later speaking with friends and family, as well as processing other evidence, the police would have to determine whether Katie was exceptionally manipulative.

Chapter 14

Unveiling
Realities Within

Shortly after being brought to the emergency room with extensive wounds, Katie Smith was pronounced dead at 12:30 P.M. The case had already caught the attention of the news media and rumors swirled. The autopsy was requested by a deputy coroner from the Kenton County Coroner's office. Another doctor and his assistant performed the autopsy. Four officers from the Fort Mitchell police department were present during the autopsy: Scott Nottingham, Tim Baringer, Marcus Best and Matt Robinson. Police anxiously awaited the results of the pathology report. Finally it came.

Significant findings of the autopsy report are:

<u>Final Anatomic Diagnosis</u>
   · Body as a Whole:
   -Multiple sharp wound injuries
   -Stab wound to the left subclavicular area with incision of major vessels.
   -Hemothorax, massive, secondary to above

-refer to comment

Comment: Death, in my judgment, is due to hypovole-mic shock due to stab wound of chest.

Identifying Marks and Scars

-A one point five centimeter scar is in the midpoint of the lower abdomen.

-A horizontal two centimeter scar is located on the upper outer quadrant of the right breast.

External/Internal Evidence of Injury

Multiple wounds are identified, first in the Emergency Room of St. Elizabeth Hospital and subsequently at the Medical Examiner's Office at St. Luke Hospital East in Ft. Thomas.

They include:

-Stab wound number one is located beneath the media aspect of the left clavicle. The wound measures two point two centimeters in length and gapes open for a space of point four centimeters. The left superior margin is sharp and trailing from this is a thin laceration. The wound does not bevel. When reapproximated it measures two point three centimeters. The wound extends through the integument, the soft tissues of the subclavicular area, and incises the lateral margin of the left subclavian/ bronchocephalic vein. This injury results in a hemothorax which is measured to be 1840 grams of liquid and clotted blood which partially fills the left pleural space.

-Wound number two is a sagitally oriented, one point five centimeter stab wound in the posterior aspect of the left arm. It is centered seven point four inches proximal to the elbow. It gapes open for a distance of point four centimeters. It has a depth of one point three centimeters. No vital structures are injured. When the wound is reapproximated it measures one point four centimeters.

-Wound labeled number three is a puncture wound over the right shoulder. It measures point two to point three centimeters in diameter.

-Wound labeled number four is a stab wound of the posterior aspect of the right shoulder. The wound measures two centimeters in length and gapes open to point five centimeters. The inferior edge is sharp. The depth of the wound is measured at six point five centimeters. It does not enter the pleural cavity. The wound reapproximates to a length of one point eight centimeters.

In addition to the wounds described above are several superficial, small, defensive type wounds noted on the palm of the left hand, and on the palm of the right hand.

A faint contusion is on the medial aspect of the right thigh.

A cluster of abrasions are over the dorsal surface of the left elbow.

SUMMARY:

Four inflicted sharp wounds are noticed. The lethal wound is a stab wound below the left clavicle which causes a massive hemothorax.

The autopsy on Katie Smith did not reveal any

reason to believe that she was or had ever been pregnant. The pathologist would not speak in absolutes due to not being able to rule out past, early term miscarriages or the possibility that Katie was only a few days pregnant. However, he was able to conclusively determine that Katie had never delivered a baby through caesarean section. The cause of death was found to be a partial severing of the superior vena cava that resulted in Katie "bleeding out" internally. In all likelihood, this occurred as a result of the first stab wound Katie received.

In addition to the autopsy report, Dr. Stephens wrote a detailed description of the heart and its function to explain Katie's demise. The superior (a) and inferior (b) vena cava are the primary veins that receive blood from the body. The superior vena cava drains the head and arms, and the inferior vena cava drains the lower body.

The right atrium receives blood from the body via the vena cavae. The atria are on the top in the heart. The blood then passes through the right atrioventricular valve which is forced shut when the ventricles contract, preventing blood from reentering the atrium. The blood goes into the right ventricle (note that it has a thinner wall; it only pumps to lungs). The ventricles are on the bottom of the heart.

The right semilunar valve marks the beginning of the artery. Again, it is supposed to close to prevent blood from flowing back into the ventricle. The pulmonary artery or pulmonary trunk is the main artery taking deoxygenated blood to the lungs.

Blood goes to the right and left lungs where

capillaries are in close contact with the thin-walled alveoli so the blood can release CO_2 and pick up O_2.

From the lungs, the pulmonary vein carries oxygenated blood back into the heart. The left atrium receives oxygenated blood from the lungs. The blood passes through the left atrioventicular valve. The blood enters the left ventricle. Note the thickened wall; the left ventricle must pump blood throughout the whole body. The blood passes through the left semilunar valve at the beginning of the aorta.

The aorta is the main artery to the body. One of the first arteries to branch off is the coronary artery, which supplies blood to the heart muscle itself so it can pump. The coronary artery goes around the heart like a crown. A blockage of the coronary artery or one of its branches is very serious, because this can cause portions of the heart to die if they don't get nutrients and oxygen. This is what occurs during a coronary heart attack. From the capillaries in the heart muscle, the blood flows back through the coronary vein, which lies on top of the artery. The aorta divides into arteries to distribute blood to the body. Small arteries are called arterioles. The smallest vessels are the capillaries. These join again to form venules, the smallest of the veins. These, in turn, join to form the larger veins, which carry the blood back to the superior and inferior vena cava.

The venous system carries the blood back to the heart. The blood flows from the capillaries, to venules (very small veins), to veins. The two largest veins in the body are the superior and inferior vena cavas. The superior vena cava carries the blood from the upper part of the body to the heart. The inferior vena cava carries the blood from the lower body to the heart. In medical terms, superior means above and inferior means under. Many people believe that the blood in the veins is blue, it is not. Venous blood is really dark red or maroon in color. Veins do have a bluish appearance and this may be why people think venous blood is blue. Both the superior and inferior vena cava end in the right atrium. The superior vena cava enters from the top and the inferior vena cava enters from the bottom.

Katie's time of death noted on the Certificate of Death was listed at 12:30 P.M. Later at the request of her family, Katie's body was cremated.

Now the physical causes of Katie's death were authenticated, but major questions were still unanswered. What had really happened at the scene of the crime and why? Was it homicide or self defense?

Chapter 15

Delving into the Facts

As conjecture and theories conflicted and grew, there was no doubt that more investigation was needed. The Fort Mitchell Police subpoenaed Katie Smith's medical records. They did not support pregnancy or any explanation for her "ailments" as being factual.

As police delved into Katie's past they found that she had claimed pregnancy three additional times, none of which resulted in a baby. Katie gave different explanations to various people of the disposition of each pregnancy. The most common explanations involved miscarriage, still-born deliveries, and death occurring shortly after birth. Family members were not allowed to attend funerals, and the one individual who Katie alleged attended a funeral claimed this to be untrue. Cemetery records revealed no infant deaths. During the course of each alleged pregnancy, family members did not accompany Katie to her doctor's appointments. When Katie claimed she was visiting doctors because of pregnancy related visits to medical facilities, treatment indicated non-pregnancy purposes for the visit. Medical records included negative pregnancy tests and provided information which would preclude pregnancy during periods of time Katie led family and friends to believe she was pregnant.

The debate on Katie Smith's state of mind and the facts about her life were leading to the theory that she may have been delusional and or had a serious personality disorder or worse.

Chapter 16

Cry Wolf?

Scott Hatton thought his brother, Aaron, was teasing him when he told Scott that Sarah had gone into labor.

Scott and Aaron were on a job site in Anderson Township, a community just east of Cincinnati. Scott, working by himself, was pouring concrete for a garage that day. In the middle of a task, his brother and a few other workers approached him.

"Sarah is about to have the baby. They're taking her to the hospital," Aaron informed Scott.

Right, Scott thought. There were numerous occasions when his co-workers received cheap thrills by crying wolf to him regarding Sarah reaching labor.

"Stop messin' with me," Scott told his brother. He was in the middle of a job and he didn't want to be distracted. Besides, he had already fallen for the joke a couple of times. He wasn't about to do it again.

"No," Aaron insisted. "Sarah's in the hospital."

"Something must have happened when she met with that woman."

"What woman?"

"That woman on the phone, the one who had the baby items for Sarah, the woman Sarah said was lonely and didn't have any friends, the woman Sarah was going to meet that morning."

That woman.

"I don't know about that, but you'd better go."

Scott immediately headed out for St. Elizabeth Medical Center in Edgewood, Kentucky, a sprawling suburban hospital at least thirty minutes from where he had been working in Ohio. As he drove, his mind raced. Fear set in.

What was going on? Was Sarah hurt? Was the baby hurt?

"I knew she was going to meet that woman," Scott said later. "But that's all I was aware of."

Meanwhile, lying in the ambulance on a stretcher, Sarah was upset, confused and scared as she worried about her baby. Why had the woman, whose name seemed to be Katie Smith, the name Sarah saw in the apartment, attack her?

"I think she wanted my baby, I think she wanted my baby," Sarah repeated in the ambulance to the attendant. "Is my baby okay? Is my baby okay?"

"Calm down," the attendant told her. "Just tell me what happened."

Fueled by adrenaline and emotion pulsing through her body, Sarah just erupted; she began gushing information, telling the horror that had taken place in Smith's apartment.

The attendant listened as the ambulance rolled into the hospital's emergency entrance.

St. Elizabeth Medical Center has more than one hundred years of history, but its sprawling south campus facility in Edgewood, Kentucky, is the epitome of a modern hospital. The staff at "St. E's," as the hospital is known in the community, is top notch, the facilities equipped with the latest in medical technology. With the future of Sarah and possibly her unborn child in jeopardy, the staff of St. E's got ready to handle the emergency.

The attention from the hospital's medical staff to Sarah was immediate. They started an IV. They cleaned and dressed Sarah's wounds. They thoroughly examined her body. Doctors asked countless questions. Nealy hovered nearby.

Because Sarah told them Katie Smith had nearly bit through Sarah's finger, the doctors asked Sarah if she recently had received a tetanus shot. Sarah also had a bite mark on her wrist and bruises on other parts of her body, but thankfully, no stab wounds.

Someone said they wanted to start taking pictures. "Whoa, wait a second," Sarah said. "I want to call somebody."

Officer Nealy told her she couldn't. Sarah responded by crying some more.

"Why can't I talk to my family? I know I didn't do anything wrong. Why can't I call somebody?" Sarah asked.

For the first time, Sarah wondered if Nealy doubted her story. But he couldn't—she was telling the truth, over and over again. He had to listen and understand.

Nealy left Sarah but quickly returned moments later.

Sarah also wanted to know what happened to Katie Smith.

"Is she here?" Sarah asked as her voice rose with anxiety.

"Yes," Nealy told her, "but don't be afraid. An officer is right outside her door and she can't get to you."

Nevertheless, discovering her attacker had been brought to the same hospital frightened Sarah. She continued to sob and desperately wanted to contact someone in her family. She needed her family now. She needed Scott. All of this was too difficult to face alone.

Nealy left the room again. A young male nurse came in. He knew Sarah was upset and must have heard her pleas to make a phone call.

"Honey," he said to Sarah, "who do you want to call?" Sarah replied, "My mom," and began rattling off the number. The nurse dialed and handed the phone to Sarah. No answer. Sarah then called her own house. Scott's mom had been staying there, and because she worked the second shift she was usually home during the day.

Again, no answer.

"So I left her this blabbering message. Who knows what I murmured. I hung up and was just crying uncontrollably because nobody was home and nobody was calling me back."

At that moment Nealy came back inside the room, holding a cell phone this time.

Nealy told Sarah it was her brother on the line, but it was actually Scott's brother.

Sarah told him everything else that happened. He couldn't believe what he heard. He tried to reassure

Sarah, told her to stay calm and then promised he'd try to reach Scott and told her that he was already on his way to the hospital with the rest of the family.

A short while later Scott arrived at the hospital.

Scott dashed into the room in a near panic. He found Sarah very, very upset. Scott noticed she had been bleeding. He began rattling off questions, wanting to know if Sarah and the baby were going to be okay.

"I still didn't have any idea what was going on," he said. "Is our baby going to live? What about the woman? Did the woman live or die? Was our baby hurt in the fight? Was she going to be normal or brain-damaged or anything like that? In a panic I was just trying to find out what was going on and trying to get a few answers."

Neither Sarah nor anyone else had reached her mother. She wanted her mother there, and didn't want any more calls until her mother was located and told about the attack.

But Sarah's medical condition needed to be monitored. The hospital staff informed Sarah that they needed to take her to labor and delivery so a doctor could check the condition of the baby. She refused a wheelchair. She wanted to walk.

They led Sarah to a small room with three beds separated by curtains. She changed into a hospital gown. Nealy continued to wander in and out of Sarah's room, asking her how she was doing. Sarah couldn't believe it. What was he thinking? Why wouldn't he leave her alone? A doctor examined Sarah and appeared surprised she was not in active labor.

The doctor advised Sarah her heartbeat was still too fast, but it was slowing down.

He decided to electronically monitor her heartbeat.

Scott came into the room and spoke with a sense of urgency.

"Sarah, you've got to call someone in your family because your story is on the news."

Sarah was taken aback, "What's on the news?"

"Your name," Scott told her. "It's all over the news."

"My name?!" Sarah couldn't believe it. "Why is my name on the news?" she murmured to herself. "I didn't do anything wrong."

"An attack like this causes people to watch," Scott said.

"Oh my God," she said. "I've got to get my mom before she hears it on the news."

Finally, a friend of Sarah's who had arrived at the hospital located Sarah's mother. To Sarah's relief, Connie Brady had not seen the story on the news. The friend told Sarah's mother what happened and assured her that Sarah and the baby were being taken care of at the hospital.

It was mid-afternoon and Sarah had not eaten since early morning. She only drank some apple juice. It had already been a long and harrowing day; Sarah wanted to go home and be safely surrounded by her family and friends.

The doctor came back in and informed Sarah of the news she wanted to hear. She was going to be discharged.

"Go home and get some rest," the doctor told her. "You've already started labor, but it's so light it could be days before you go into full term labor."

Scott, in disbelief, wanted to know why the doctor

just didn't perform a Caesarean and take the baby right then. After all, Sarah had started labor, (even though it was mild and in the very early stages) and was already in the hospital.

"No," the doctor explained, "I'm going to let her do it by herself. I'm going to let her body do it, it's safer."

Officer Nealy returned to the room. This time two other officers, Detective Scott Nottingham and Sergeant Tom Loos, accompanied him. Sarah could immediately tell that Nealy's demeanor had changed. He had been so nice and under-standing. Now, he appeared more serious, even agitated.

As he watched anxiously, Scott remembers that the first thing the police asked was to take a look at Sarah's hands. Scott calculated they were checking her wounds to help determine that her recollection of the fight matched the defensive wounds she suffered.

Then, one of the officers asked Sarah, "Why did you think that woman was pregnant?"

Sarah looked at Scott. She was confused and a little thrown by the strange query.

"What do you mean, why do I think she was pregnant? Because she is pregnant," Sarah told the police.

"Well," one of the cops said "we have reason to believe that she isn't, or if she is, it could be only a couple of weeks."

Sarah began getting upset again. "No, this lady was nine months pregnant like me. She said she was going to be induced today. I'm not crazy."

The police were emphatic. No, they insisted, the woman was not pregnant. "Could she have had a shirt or something stuffed inside of her sweatshirt to make it look like she was nine months pregnant?" the officer asked.

"I don't see how. She looked as big if not bigger than me," Sarah responded. Sarah's mind raced. What did they mean, the woman wasn't pregnant? Sarah saw her, the nursery, the baby clothes, formula and gifts. Sarah talked to her about pregnancy. She, like Sarah, was about to have a baby. The woman had talked of little else. What was going on here?

It was then that Sergeant Loos delivered more startling news to Sarah.

"Sarah, she died."

Sarah sat motionless and emotionless, overwhelmed with shock and disbelief.

Officer Nealy gave this account of his interview with Sarah Brady at the hospital:

Arriving at St. Elizabeth Medical Center, I spoke with Sarah regarding what happened. Sarah gave the following account of incidents that occurred during the attack:

On Tuesday February 8, 2005 around 4:10 P.M. Sarah received a call from an unnamed woman looking for her. Sarah told her that she was about to leave assuming the woman was a bill collector. She talked to the woman for a couple of minutes, took a message and hung up.

On Wednesday February 9, 2005 around 12:00 P.M. the same woman called Sarah at home. The woman identified herself as Sarah Brody, (later identified as Katie Smith), and said she received some packages from Babies-R-Us. She explained that once she opened the packages she noticed they were intended for a Sarah Brady. She asked Ms. Brady if she was pregnant and if she was registered with Babies-R-Us. The woman said that she believed that the packages were sent to the wrong person and wanted to know if Sarah would like to stop by and pick them up. Sarah Brady told her she would pick them up.

On Wednesday February 9, 2005 around 12:45 P.M. Sarah Brady went to Katie Smith's apartment and met with Katie. Katie gave her a Babies-R-Us bag with bottle covers, nipples, a baby blanket, diapers and a headrest for a car seat. Ms. Brady said she stayed for about thirty minutes. Katie told Sarah that she was married and her husband was out of town on business. Katie explained that they had just moved here from St. Louis and she didn't have any friends in the area. She was supposed to be induced for delivery on Thursday. Sarah took the items and put them in the front seat of her Jeep and left.

On Wednesday February 9, 2005 around 7:30 or 8:00 P.M. Katie called and said she had received another package containing a Fischer Price Swing Along. They talked for about forty-five minutes and agreed to meet around 9:00 A.M. on Thursday.

On Thursday February 10, 2005, Sarah Brady went to Smith's apartment to pick up the baby swing. Katie gave Sarah the swing and said she couldn't find the invoice for it. Katie also presented Sarah with a tour of the apartment and nursery. They discussed baby items and where to register online for free gifts. Katie handed Sarah some coupons for free baby formula. The name *Katie Smith* was printed on the coupons. They continued to look for the invoice for the swing while Sarah noticed an inhaler on the bedroom nightstand with the name Katie Smith on it. Sarah said she started to get a bad feeling about what was happening and intended to leave the apartment. She got her keys from her pocket and told Katie that she needed to head off. As Sarah tried to exit the front door she noticed it was locked. Katie pretended to have pain and thought she was going into labor. Sarah told her she needed to call her doctor right away and Katie went into the bedroom. Sarah said it sounded like Katie was carrying on a conversation with her doctor. When the call was finished, Sarah tried to leave again. Katie came over and hugged Sarah and then pulled a knife out of her sweatshirt pocket. A struggle began and Sarah grabbed the knife from Katie and accidentally dropped it on the floor. Sarah remembered struggling with Katie, knocking over a table and trying to get to the door. At one point, Sarah exited the apartment door to the breeze-way and Katie pulled her back into the apartment by grabbing her hair. Sarah said she was screaming for help and Katie told her there was no one nearby that could hear her. Sarah was in fear for her life and stabbed Katie. After Sarah stabbed Katie, she fell on the couch. Sarah grabbed a portable phone and ran outside attempting to dial 911.

Once outside, a woman with her young daughter stopped to help Sarah and told her she would dial 911 once she returned home. I arrived shortly afterwards.

The story Nealy documented from Sarah's hospital bed still needed to be verified and more facts ascertained.

Chapter 17

Murder or Self Defense?

The police continued to question Sarah despite her condition.

They took thirty photographs of Sarah's wounds. She suffered injuries to her left hand, left palm, left forearm, right wrist, right ring finger, right elbow, left and right side of her face.

Sarah's story was supported by matching defensive wounds characteristic of the fight she described and by injuries which appeared to be consistent with her story of disarming a knife-wielding Katie with her bare hands.

Both Scott and Sarah were physically and emotionally exhausted by the time the police officers finished photo-graphing Sarah's wounds.

Scott broke down into tears as Sarah sat numbly in shock at Officer Loos' revelation about the woman's death. Looking over at Scott, she began crying while Scott continued to sob.

"Get the hell out of her room!" Scott demanded in

response to the police officer's insensitive questioning.

Scott was angry and upset with how the police were treating Sarah. Were they insinuating that Sarah killed the woman? He didn't understand.

"Leave her room! Get out! Get out of her room now!" Scott demanded.

Nealy tried to calm down both of them.

"Is she under arrest?" Scott wanted to know.

Nealy looked first at Sarah, then at Scott before speaking. "Not yet."

"Not yet! Oh my God," Sarah cried out, "You're going to arrest me for killing that woman!"

Sarah remembered stabbing Katie, but it was in the shoulder. Sarah didn't think it was worse than a shallow wound.

"How did she die of that?" Sarah agonized.

Through cascading tears, Sarah repeated over and over, "I didn't want her to die. I wasn't trying to kill her. I wasn't trying to make her die. I just wanted to escape."

Scott, the hard-nosed construction worker and former star athlete, was still bawling.

Sarah later asked him if he was he worried or pissed off.

"Both," Scott said reflectively. "I kept thinking, 'Is this really happening? Am I awake?'"

The police continued to prod Sarah, wanting to know why she didn't show more emotion after learning she had taken a life.

"They just came in and told me I killed somebody," Sarah later said. "I kept asking them what they were talking about. It was like they dropped a bombshell and I was already in shock and then I felt completely traumatized."

Looking at the couple appraisingly, Nealy realized the gravity of the situation and how the news about Katie's death stunned and upset Scott and Sarah. He softened his approach.

"I'm sorry," Nealy told Sarah. "I know you're in shock. This is a whole lot for you. But I need you to come to the police station."

"No she's not!" Scott snapped. "She's not. She's had nothing to eat, no sleep. She needs to go home and go to sleep. She doesn't need to answer any more questions. You'll need to wait until the morning."

Nealy pleaded his case for conducting a more formal interview at the Fort Mitchell Police Station.

"Sarah, if you do it now, it's going to be fresh in your memory," Nealy encouraged her.

Scott continued to argue against an interview. Family members began coming in. Sarah got up to change her clothes. The debate over the interview continued. One of the doctors came in and told Sarah she could leave the hospital and go home.

Finally, as she was preparing to leave, Sarah looked at Nealy and agreed to the interview.

"I'm coming," she said. Sarah was confident she had done nothing wrong, and she wanted to make sure the police knew that.

"No, no you're not," Scott said.

"Yes I am," she told Scott. "I remember everything. I have nothing to hide. I want to tell them what I know."

Later, Sarah would explain that the police wanted to determine if she knew Katie died after the fight.

"I didn't think she was dead," Sarah said. "We

struggled over the knife and I stabbed her in the shoulder. I knew she was wounded, but I didn't think she was going to die."

Meanwhile, Sarah's family had gathered in the hospital waiting room. Little by little they began piecing together what had happened and eventually heard on the radio that the pregnant woman had died.

While talking, they were approached by a heavyset woman who was part of a group of people also in the waiting room.

Sarah's family was startled when the woman told them, "Shut the hell up, you're upsetting everybody!"

One of Sarah's family members walked over to a security guard and reported the incident. He separated the two groups. Sarah's family surmised they must have been family members of the woman who died.

Scott's sister-in-law offered to drive Scott and Sarah to the police station. They followed the police on the quick route to Fort Mitchell. It was close to 4:00 P.M. and Sarah was physically and emotionally exhausted, but she wanted to explain exactly what occurred in the corner apartment.

In her mind, telling the truth would clear up any suspicions about what really took place in the attack. It did not even occur to her to contact a lawyer. The police did give Sarah a warning about the press, telling her lots of TV cameras would be at the police station. They advised her to keep her head down and just keep walking. They told Sarah, "The reporters will shout questions, but you don't have to say anything."

Sarah soon learned about the insatiable appetite the media and the public had for the sensational story of a mother protecting her unborn child from a woman so desperate she is willing to kill for the baby.

Sure enough, the media was waiting. As instructed, Sarah kept her head down and hustled past the line of reporters. Once inside the station, which was just around the corner from the apartment where the woman died, the police informed Sarah they would need more photos of her.

The police told Sarah that they conferred with doctors at the hospital and determined that Sarah was wounded in self defense while fighting off Smith's attacks. This helped confirm Sarah's recollection of the battle.

Sarah, Scott, Nealy and Detective Nottingham went into a room. The police wanted to tape the interview. Sarah didn't object.

They talked for a while; the police continued firing questions at Sarah. She answered every inquiry and once again took the officers through the events which occurred earlier that afternoon at the apartment.

During the questioning Nottingham was called out of the room. He returned a few moments later and looked at Sarah.

"An attorney has been called for you. He's on his way."

What attorney? Sarah thought to herself. She didn't call an attorney and wasn't even thinking about doing so. She didn't need an attorney. After all, she was telling the simple truth. Why should she have to defend herself?

What Sarah didn't know was that Ron Hatton, who had been waiting outside the interview room, had grown anxious and nervous, because the interview was taking so long. Through some mutual friends Scott's brother was given the name of Bob Carran, one of the area's top criminal defense lawyers.

Carran told Ron to tell Sarah to stop answering questions and to let her know that he was on his way. At that point, the interview stopped. However, Sarah had already given the police plenty of information. Soon the attorney arrived.Bob Carran comes over as an intellectual. He's tall and fashionably thin, wears thin-framed glasses and is always dressed in a well cut suit. His serious demeanor belies a very good sense of humor and a keen mind. Carran is the type of able lawyer who clients call when they need top legal representation.

Carran told Sarah they needed to talk alone. He and Sarah went into a larger conference-style room so they could be alone. Carran began questioning his new prospective client.

Have you ever been arrested?

"No."

Are you on any medication?

"No."

Do you have any past history of violence?

Again, Sarah answered, "No."

Finally, Carran bluntly asked Sarah about the attack. "Did you do it?"

"No!" Sarah's voice rose sincerely. "She wanted my baby and tried to kill me!"

"All right," Carran said, apparently satisfied Sarah was telling the truth. "Let's go back in."

The questioning resumed, but after about fifteen

minutes Carran and Nottingham stood up and left the room together. They returned half an hour later.

"Sarah, you don't need me," Carran said. "You don't have anything to worry about. You're not going to need any legal advice. They know it was self-defense. They just want a statement from you."

During the entire interview, before and after Carran arrived, the police were very nice, a change from how tough they had acted at the hospital when they told Sarah about Smith's death. Maybe it was a "good cop, bad cop" act, Sarah thought, but now that they were sure she was telling the truth she felt relaxed.

The truth they say is easy to remember. Police know this maxim too.

The police did question Sarah as to why she thought the woman was pregnant. Sarah repeated over and over how the woman looked heavy and appeared to be nine months pregnant and how all the things in the apartment caused Sarah to believe she was preparing to have a baby.

"I went through the whole story, detail by detail. I never felt like anything I was telling them was wrong. I was telling them the truth."

At the end of the interview, Detective Nottingham turned off the tape recorder and looked Sarah in the eye.

"I want you to know that we know you acted in self-defense. You did not do anything wrong. We know you were protecting yourself and your baby. And there's nothing wrong with that."

Nottingham also interviewed Scott.

When Scott spoke to Nottingham, he described

Sarah as being passive and non-aggressive with a calm, relaxed demeanor. Scott notes that he is the disciplinarian regarding his son. Sarah refuses to spank him and limits her discipline to time-outs. Scott said that Sarah is not adventurous, prefers to be around family and has nurtured his son as if he were her own child. He then spoke of Sarah's charity work, specifically the annual tradition of obtaining a needy child's information from the Christmas tree on Fountain Square in Cincinnati, Ohio. Scott told me that even though the child's card might ask for socks or gloves, she would also get a toy for the child. He said Sarah does this so that there will be one less child who has to have a Christmas similar to those of her own childhood.

Nottingham inquired as to why Scott and Sarah were not married. Scott explained that it was due to lack of money. He said that they were waiting to save enough to put a down payment on a house and pay for a wedding.

Sarah finally left the police station for the drive home. Though she felt her own innocence had to be believed, she would remember the horror of what Katie Smith had tried to do and the savagery of what had happened for the rest of her life. Though relieved, she now felt mentally and physically drained. But Sarah felt sure that she convinced the police to believe the truth of her story. And she thanked God that her baby would be okay.

Sarah and Scott went home as evening descended. Several friends and family came over to talk and comfort her. Later that night as Sarah showered, all the fear and terror she'd experienced flooded back. She wanted the water to wash away all the evil which hammered at her body that day in the attack. She couldn't even comb her hair because of the knots tangled in her curls. Her body ached and throbbed with pain as she lay down in bed. She could not sleep. She lay awake in the darkness agonizing about the strange events that had occurred and wondered why. Scott held her as she cried. He tried to soothe Sarah by telling her there was nothing she could have done to change the ending of what had happened. Sarah felt better when later that night Scott comforted her. "Sarah, you didn't take her life; she took her own."

Sarah prayed all night long. She even prayed for Katie Smith's soul.

Chapter 18

Accusations

Just two days after Sarah Brady killed Katie Smith when she was trying to take Sarah's life and her baby, Katie Smith's family apologized profusely.

That's the message Detective Nottingham relayed to Sarah when he talked to her.

Nottingham had called to ask Sarah a few more questions about the attack, including what Katie Smith was wearing during the fight. After they had been talking a few minutes, Nottingham told her that members of Smith's family wanted to offer their sympathy.

"They hope that the baby is going to be okay and they are really sorry that this happened," Nottingham said, according to Sarah's recollection of the conversation. "Obviously it's awkward. They can't contact you directly and tell you these things because they're also grieving."

In response, a day later, during an interview, Sarah

expressed sympathy for Smith's family.

"I did feel for the family. Regardless of what she did to me, they still lost part of their family."

Gradually, though, as more information about Katie Smith's savage plan came out, Sarah had increased animosity about the woman who attacked her.

About a month later, Chief Hensley and Detective Nottingham paid a visit to Scott's mother's house to talk to Sarah about information that Smith had possibly been stalking her prior to the attack.

Incredibly, the police had mail from Scott and Sarah's home that had been found in Katie Smith's apartment. Sarah immediately knew it was her mail. One of the pieces of mail was a sanitation bill from January. Scott was selling a car in January and Sarah had written a message from a prospective buyer on the envelope. A cold chill came over Sarah. How did Katie Smith get her mail? Did she break into Sarah and Scott's home prior to the attack? Had she been watching Sarah? If so, for how long?

"It creeped me out thinking she was following me, stalking me," Sarah later said.

The police said Smith may have gotten the mail out of Sarah's car. That was unlikely, Sarah said, since she doesn't remember ever putting the mail in her green Jeep Cherokee SUV.

Either way, Katie Smith had obviously picked her target well before the attack. By stealing mail, Katie had Sarah's name. The fact that Katie already knew Sarah's name made it easier for her to look Sarah up on the Toys R Us website and resulted in Katie choosing the phony name of Sarah Brody.

Once Sarah found out that Smith's attack was proving to be more methodical and planned than she first believed, she felt it was no accident that Smith was trolling through the baby gift registry and just happened upon Sarah. The mail provided evidence that Smith was likely stalking Sarah, possibly for weeks before the attack.

Looking back, there were other signs at the time that were unexplained, but given what happened they were starting to make more sense.

For instance, on at least two occasions there was an indication someone had gotten into Sarah and Scott's home. Sarah's sister had been coming over to clean the house during the late stages of Sarah's pregnancy.

"She told me a few times when she came in the back door was standing open," Sarah said. "We wondered if somebody had broken in, but nothing was missing." Still, a deranged stranger being in the home disturbed Sarah and left her shaken.

She could not help thinking of other disquieting incidents. Another time, Sarah had asked Aaron's girlfriend to come over because she was sure she had heard someone in the upstairs of the house.

"Looking back now," Sarah said, "that was just all too weird."

Further troubling to her, Sarah also learned more about Smith's past dealings with children.

Smith was babysitting, acting as a nanny of sorts, for two northern Kentucky families. The father of one of the families was a doctor. One day the woman of the other family came home to find Smith loading the children into a car. Smith said she was going to take them over the doctor's house to play with his kids.

The woman was upset. Smith had specific instructions not to take the children anywhere. Sarah could not help wondering if she was going to let the kids have some play time, or if she had something more dangerous in mind.

The woman had fired Smith the next day.

But the police hadn't come to visit Sarah that day to talk about Smith. They wanted to give Sarah news she was hardly expecting, news that would, as she later put it, leave her "flabbergasted."

The police weren't closing the case.

They launched into a more disturbing line of questioning.

Some of Smith's family had suddenly claimed that Sarah was arranging to sell her baby. Smith, her family believed, was working as a baby broker and had arranged to "buy" Sarah's daughter for $5,000. The cash, at least according to the family members, had been paid to Sarah over time. The relatives told police they had periodically given money, a few hundred dollars at a time, to Katie, and she had been paying that money to Sarah. The plan was for Sarah to go to Katie's apartment. Using the surgical tools police found, Katie would deliver the baby and then "resell" the infant on the black market.

The allegations continued. According to them, when Sarah arrived at Smith's apartment, Sarah changed her mind. Sarah didn't want to give up her baby or pay back the five thousand dollars. So Sarah killed Smith and made up the story about the fight.

There was more. Someone, Sarah heard (she was not

sure who), reported seeing a green Jeep SUV just like Sarah's several times in Smith's neighborhood prior to the attack.

"We have to look at this," the police told Sarah.

Sarah was speechless. Was this really happening? She had nearly lost her life and her baby in a fight with a woman that probably had been stalking her for some time, and now the police were investigating whether Sarah actually wanted to sell her baby. The very thought of doing something like that, coupled with the fact the police were now questioning her about it, made her sick to her stomach.

When the police first visited her to discuss the allegations, Sarah was astonished. "I was sitting there with a blank stare and said to the cops, 'Are you serious!? That makes no sense because I'm not the kind of person who's going to sell her baby.'"

One of the officers cut in, agreeing that Sarah did not fit the profile of a baby seller. "The price is usually $10,000 or more for a baby sold on the black market. Typically, it's a single mom who hasn't told anyone about her pregnancy who is willing to partake in the dreadful and disturbing act of selling a newborn child like it's a piece of merchandise."

"I had the complete opposite situation," Sarah objected. But again, the police said they had to investigate the Smith family's allegations.

"I was floored," Sarah said. "Where are those people that felt sorry for me? I almost lost my life and my baby's life, and now they are trying to say I wanted to sell my baby."

Sarah felt like she was being cast as the villain even

after all the information she had given the police.

"Katie Smith's not the victim," Sarah told the police. "I don't care which way you look at it. Yes, she is dead, but I'm the victim. I'm the one that has to live with this for the rest of my life. I didn't do this to her, she did this to me."

Sarah challenged the police's assertions and speculation.

"Check my phone records. Other than the calls she made to me, you'll find nothing. Give me dates and times when somebody said they saw my Jeep, and I'll tell you where I was. I was probably working. There are a lot of green Jeep Cherokees. What proof is there that it was mine?"

Sarah claims that when the police subsequently did check the records, they confirmed Sarah's story. There wasn't any proof that Katie Smith and Sarah had talked to one another prior to the week of the attack.

Sarah felt mortified that the police were even pursuing the notion that she wanted to sell her baby. The entire time they had been telling her that she wouldn't be arrested, that she had acted in self-defense, and they believed her story.

And why wouldn't they believe it? Sarah was completely certain that she had been consistent in her recollection of events, and she never strayed from the story she told the EMS attendant right after the attack while they were riding in the ambulance to the hospital.

"How can someone be so together, tell the same story in the ambulance, in the police station, to medical personnel, to attorneys, and have made it all up? How did I come up with something so quickly? How did I come up with all of this as I was going into cardiac arrest riding in the ambulance on the way to the hospital, and then stick to the same story each time I told it after that?"

"I'll tell you how—because that's what happened. I told the truth the entire time. It never changed *because* it was the truth. There's not even a circumstantial bit of evidence to support what Katie's family is saying."

Bill Crockett, the Kenton County prosecutor, was interviewed by Keith Olbermann of MSNBC after the attack. John Osterhage, who prosecuted Katie Smith's father, works for Bill Crockett's office.

"Brady says it was maternal instinct that enabled her to save herself," Olbermann said in relating the story on his popular "Countdown" cable television program. "While police contend that the evidence points toward self-defense, local authorities are still deciding whether or not to press charges against Sarah Brady, and they're discussing the possibility of taking the case to a grand jury."

Olbermann then directed his questions at Crockett, an intelligent low-key lawyer known for his laid-back demeanor.

"I'm sure a lot of viewers would be surprised to hear that there is still a possibility that Ms. Brady will be charged," Olbermann said. "Is that because of facts not yet publicly known, or is it just standard procedure? What is it?"

Crockett said his interest in the case was "standard procedure," and that the public, through television and the media, is used to instant gratification when it comes to solving crimes and closing cases.

"What we're looking at (is) society by virtue of forty-five second news clips here and there and forty-five minutes to solve every major crime in 'CSI' and every other network television show," Crockett said. "There is, I guess, a perception that you can resolve these things instantly. In this particular case, we have to follow up on every lead, forensic, factual and other bases. And that's what we're in the process of doing right now."

Olbermann asked, point blank, if there was any evidence to suggest that Sarah was not telling the truth.

"Everything that Ms. Brady has told the police to this point has been confirmed," Crockett admitted to Olbermann. "But again, we have to explore it. Obviously, we're not in a position to accept at face value the statement of any person who has been involved in a fatality."

Sarah, who had been through so much pain and turmoil, was still dealing with the lingering anxiety of the attack: sleepless nights, crying days, and recurring paranoia. Now she had to worry about the police still doubting her story.

It wasn't going to be easy to handle.

Chapter 19

Bizarre Truths and Blatant Lies

Scott and Sarah were at Scott's grandmother's home on Saturday morning trying to regain the normalcy of their lives. They both asked themselves if that would ever be possible again. There was no way to erase what happened. Sarah had killed a woman who had tried to steal her unborn child in a vicious hand-to-hand battle. The media and internet broadcasted the story all over the country and the world. Thousands and thousands of hits appeared on Google. Caught in the turmoil, Sarah and Scott didn't know how they were ever going to be able to put this behind them and move on.

Sarah's sister flew in from California to help Sarah. Family members and the lawyers tried their best to keep the media hounds at bay. Sarah and Scott encouraged each other to focus on the impending birth of their daughter.

That, Sarah thought to herself, *will make our situation better*. We'll be able to think about something hopeful, something upbeat, and not dwell on my savage encounter with Katie Smith.

Then the phone rang. It was the police.

"Now what?" Sarah murmured while listening to the voice on the other end of the line. She took the call out of curiosity.

"We need to ask you a few more questions regarding what happened," the officer said.

"What was Katie wearing?"

Sarah thought to herself, *Well, you should know.* Were the police trying to catch her in a lie? Trip her up? Confuse her? What was this all about? I've done nothing wrong, Sarah told herself, the truth is easy to remember.

"Her pajamas and sweatshirt from the day before when I had been there, the same exact outfit," Sarah said. "I assume they were her pajamas."

"Did the sweatshirt have a pocket?"

"Yeah," Sarah said. "I've already told you this in the interview."

The police officers then began questioning Sarah in regards to the 911 calls she made from Katie Smith's apartment.

"Did you ever call 911? Why didn't you try?"

Sarah grew agitated. Through her mind spun the vision of how she had clutched Katie Smith's phone during the brutal fight.

"I did call, twice," she told the officer. "I tried to call twice. I tried to call inside the apartment and outside the apartment. I don't know if either of the calls went through."

"Those calls went through," the police officer said.

"It's probably how the police were first alerted to a problem at the apartment and how Hensley arrived so quickly on the scene the day of the fight."

Sarah also heard from someone, maybe it was on the news, that another 911 call came from a different number. Sarah believes it was Katie Smith calling 911 on her cell phone.

Police later confirmed that four 911 calls were made. However, only three were long enough to transcribe. Even as Katie Smith lay mortally wounded, she was lying to an emergency operator about how the attack really occurred.

The first 911 call transcript released by the Fort Mitchell Police Department illustrates the amazing effect to which Sarah pushed herself:

BRADY: Help!
DISPATCHER: KENTON COUNTY 911
BRADY: Help!
DISPATCHER: What's the problem ma'am?
BRADY: Help!
DISPATCHER: Don't know what's going on, she kept yelling 'help' and the line disconnected.

From this dispatch call, it's unclear whether Sarah understood the dispatcher's questions. The dispatcher through the hysteria, was unable to decipher whether the voice was male or female.

The second 911 call came from the lady who, along with her young daughter, saw Sarah frantically trying to get help. The woman told Fort Mitchell Police Sergeant,

Jim Bussman, that she was driving her car nearby Katie Smith's apartment when she saw a lady (Sarah) dressed in all black trying to flag her down. Sarah, the woman reported, was in the middle of the street seeking assistance. The woman, though worried about the safety of her daughter, was concerned enough about Sarah to stop her car and offer her assistance by dialing 911. The following is the transcript of the second 911 call:

DISPATCHER: KENTON COUNTY 911
WOMAN: Hi, I was calling because there is a lady...
DISPATCHER: Uh, huh
WOMAN: Screaming for help
DISPATCHER: Okay, we got a call from her on 911 and I'm trying to figure out what's going on, do you know any further?
WOMAN: No.
DISPATCHER: Okay. Is she outside?
WOMAN: Yes
DISPATCHER: What was she wearing?
WOMAN: All black. I mean I can go back up there...
DISPATCHER: Okay, I think we've got another call and we are attempting to figure out what is going on.
DISPATCHER: And she is outside of her apartment.
WOMAN: She's up at the top of the hill...
DISPATCHER: Tell me what she looks like, what color hair?
WOMAN: Black, it's curly and shoulder length. And she's got this black kind of dressy shirt on, black dress pants.
DISPATCHER: Can I get a call back number for you?

WOMAN: Yes.
DISPATCHER: Okay, we're sending them out. Thank you.
WOMAN: Uh, huh.
DISPATCHER: Bye.
WOMAN: Bye.

The transcript reveals that the police remained understandably confused regarding the situation. However, the dispatcher sent the police out to the apartment.

The third and final 911 call came from Katie Smith. It is perhaps the most revealing of how deeply delusional she was even as she uttered her dying words:

DISPATCHER: KENTON COUNTY 911
SMITH: Help me. I've been stabbed.
DISPATCHER: Okay, Who stabbed you?
SMITH: A woman, she broke in.
DISPATCHER: Who broke in?
SMITH: Her name is Sarah.
DISPATCHER: Where are you bleeding from ma'am?
SMITH: I don't know, I can't see (can't understand???)
DISPATCHER: Is she still there?
SMITH: (can't understand???)
DISPATCHER: Okay, the police are on their way over there. We've got the squad started. You are at your apartment on the first floor. Ma'am...(Unrelated Conversation Deleted)... Hello...(Unrelated Conversation Deleted)...Hello...Hello...Are you inside your house? Okay, you are inside your residence

ma'am? Ma'am? Ma'am? (Unrelated Conversation Deleted)

As she lay dying, Katie Smith accused Sarah of breaking into her home. The last words on the tape from Katie Smith clearly reflect Katie is losing consciousness and fails to utter anything comprehensible. According to Kenton County Commonwealth Attorney Bill Crockett and Fort Mitchell Police Chief Steve Hensley, there is what appears to be gurgling in Katie Smith's throat. They surmise it is blood.

Sarah Brady did not know it, but her 911 call did go through and the only thing audible on the recording is Sarah Brady hysterically screaming for help. After a few minutes delay, Katie Smith calls 911 claiming that someone named Sarah broke into her apartment and stabbed her. However, the police later fail to notice any signs of forced entry. A time line was assembled with regards to the 911 calls and the police and EMS dispatch times. The police created the time line because Sarah Brady claimed to have been attacked by a pregnant woman, yet Katie Smith did not appear to be pregnant. Katie was found wearing only a blood stained sweatshirt and panties. A pair of bloody maternity underwear stuffed with padding and pajama type pants would later be located in a closet. The time line clearly demonstrated that Katie had enough time after Sarah fled her apartment to remove the clothing, hide it in the closet and then make her 911 call. The amazing thing was that though she was gravely wounded, her resolve was so strong and demented that she found the strength to continue her diabolical plan.

Police Summary of Time line of 911 and Dispatch Calls

11:30:51-
11:32:00   The first 911 call is received from Sarah Brady on the home cordless telephone as she exited Katie Smith's apartment and began heading towards Dixie highway. Heavy breathing, and screams for help can be heard by Dispatcher West. Total call time: Sixty-nine seconds.

11:31:51 Fort Mitchell Police are dispatched to Katie Smith's apartment.

11:32:09-
11:32:20 The second 911 call is received from Sarah Brady on the home cordless telephone. The line disconnects prior to anything being heard by Dispatcher West. Total call time: Eleven seconds.

11:33:51-
11:35:33 The third 911 call is received from the woman who helped Sarah Brady on her home phone. She tells Dispatcher West that she saw Sarah Brady on the sidewalk near Dixie Highway screaming for help. Total call time: 102 seconds.

11:33:53-
11:35:11 The fourth 911 calls is received from Katie Smith on her cellular phone. Katie Smith asks Dispatcher Richter for help and tells her that she has been stabbed by a woman named 'Sarah'.

Total call time: Seventy-eight seconds

11:35:41 Fort Mitchell Police Officer, Scott Nealy locates Sarah Brady at the corner of Dixie Highway.

11:36:00 Fort Mitchell Police Officers Roy Taylor and Sergeant Jim Bussman arrive at Smith's apartment and locate Katie Smith.

11:37:47 Fort Mitchell Life Squad Fourteen arrives at Katie Smith's apartment.

11:38:xx Fort Mitchell Life Squad Sixteen arrives near Dixie Highway.

Note-Kenton County Dispatch Supervisor Billy Snipes verified that all 911 calls received are docu-mented on both the 911 call log and on the call audit trail. There weren't any calls received on any other line by the Kenton County Dispatch Center, which does not explain the discrepancies between the audio recordings and the log.

Police eventually surmised that Katie located Sarah through the Babies 'R Us website registration. The company issued this curt statement following the attack:

"We place the highest priority on respecting the privacy of all our guests. We recognize the serious nature of the situation and are actively investigating this matter."

Later that night, Sarah and Scott watched a report about the attack on the television news. What they heard and saw was another stunning revelation that they had not been told by the police.

The reporter announced that in the search of Katie

Smith's apartment, police found what was described as a pregnancy suit. Sarah and Scott stared in horror as an image of the suit flashed on the screen. It was underwear stuffed with some sort of synthetic padding.

Blood was splattered on the crude outfit.

Sarah and Scott were speechless for several moments. "Oh my God," Sarah finally said.

Sarah deduced the police decided not to inform her about the suit to test her veracity and determine if her story was consistent through the many times she had already told it.

Other bits of reality were beginning to surface. One theory was that the woman apparently planned to not only kill Sarah, but also to immediately deliver her baby and keep it for herself. No one Katie Smith knew would be suspicious, because she had pulled off her pregnancy ruse; people thought her pregnant. She was wearing maternity clothes, and if she showed up with a baby, they would believe it was hers. Sick, but simple.

In horror, Sarah now saw what the police had taken into custody the day of the attack. There were surgical scissors, clamps, a clip used to cut an umbilical cord and rubber gloves found in Smith's apartment. The reporter revealed that these allegedly were the tools she planned to use in her devious and macabre delivery of Sarah's baby.

Not long afterwards, Sarah also learned the probable scenario of the moments after she saved her life, and her baby's life.

Smith had been stabbed three times in the fight with Sarah: in the upper part of her chest, in the back of her right shoulder and the upper left shoulder.

Dazed, bleeding and close to passing out, Katie Smith made her way from the apartment's living room to her bedroom. Somehow summoning her remaining strength, she shed the homemade pregnancy suit, stuffed it in a closet and changed clothes.

Police found Katie Smith lying dead in her blood-splattered apartment. She was twenty-two years old and childless.

As more and more of the bizarre facts came out, Sarah learned Katie Smith had never been married. She was unemployed and was not pursuing any career. Sarah found out Katie's desire for a child was so deep and psychotic that she had evidently hatched and started to carry out a plot to kill a woman nine months pregnant and take the baby for her own. The woman she had fastened on was Sarah.

The horrifying elements were mind-boggling. The question, which plagued Sarah and the public as they learned the details of the savage crime, was the same one:

How did Katie Smith reach this diabolical point in her life?

Chapter 20

A Dysfunctional Family

Independence, Kentucky, is directly in the middle of Kenton County, the state's third largest county and a place of diverse geography, communities and population. Long and skinny, the county runs from the Ohio River at the state's northernmost point through urban neighborhoods, affluent suburbs, booming suburbs, sleepy farming communities and rolling farm land where horses, cows and tobacco share space in the county's far south end.

Independence, the county seat, is both a little country town as well as one of the fastest growing cities in the state. While subdivisions bulging with young families have taken the place of livestock and crops on what was once fertile farmland, the city still has a small town feel. A historic courthouse, a Rockwellian business district and a sprawling cemetery that covers both sides of the main road, give way to the new shopping center, grocery store, schools, restaurants, police station, parks, senior citizen center and sidewalks that have followed the new residents to town.

Patriotic holidays in a place called Independence are a major happening. Every Memorial Day there is a parade; Fourth of July heralds another parade, a day-long festival and a fireworks display to conclude the festivities.

Traveling just south of town one sees the landscape rapidly morphing into the characteristics associated with "the country"—curvy roads, deep woods, picturesque farms, quaint churches, a drag strip for the local hot rods, a country store at a state route crossroads, the county fairgrounds where the demolition derby always draws big crowds and the Licking River lazily rolling by places with names like Morningview, Ryland, Visalia and White Villa.

It was in this seemingly tranquil and even enviable environment that Katie Smith was born and raised.

But there was nothing enviable or tranquil about Katie Smith's childhood.

Katie's parents, Tim and Cindy Smith, met in 1974 and were married in 1976. Together, they had five girls. The family often traveled on family camping trips to lakes and parks across the state, including Kentucky Lake and Lake Cumberland. Tim Smith often boasted about all of his girls being intelligent and outgoing.

Katie was the second oldest of five girls. The oldest was born in 1978 followed by Katie in 1983. Three younger girls completed the family. Katie attended the area high school, Simon Kenton High School. This school is named for the famous Kentucky pioneer, Simon Kenton, who wrongly believed he killed a man in

Virginia and fled to Kentucky. Among his many exploits, Simon Kenton once saved the better-known Daniel Boone from being killed by Indians by throwing Boone on his back and carrying him to safety. A rural high school consistent with the area had grown by the year 2005 to accommodate 1,400 students. As the town of Independence has grown, so has Simon Kenton.

After attending Simon Kenton, Katie also attended but did not remain at Midway College, a small school in central Kentucky near Lexington.

In 1996 Tim Smith's mother moved from Palm Springs, California and came to live with the Smith family. From 1976 to 1992, Tim Smith worked for a painting contractor. From 1976 to 2000, Katie's mother worked at Downing Displays in Cincinnati.

Katie's parents both had serious problems with alcohol misuse. Whether her father was much worse is an issue debated within the family. Katie's aunt remembered Katie as a talkative, happy, vibrant child. Her uncle recalls Katie as an intelligent and articulate girl. However, they both agree she longed for attention and would stretch the truth to draw attention.

According to one story she allegedly told in the eighth grade and high school, Katie claimed to some kids that she had Lupus, a kidney disease, and feigned fibromyalgia and panic attacks.

Simon Kenton students and former classmates remember Katie as "always a little odd."

"I used to work at a toy store and she would come in there all the time saying she was pregnant," one former student recalled in the posting, adding that Katie never did come in with a baby or child. "However, a few years back she brought two garbage bags full of baby items and tried to return them. When she said she had miscarried twins, she was given approval to return her products."

"She always did have an obsession with children, but I never would have imagined her trying to steal someone else's (baby) from their womb," the classmate wrote.

Another student said, "Katie was made fun of in high school for wearing maternity clothes all the time," according to a posting on the Internet forum. "So I guess this is something she always wanted. The whole thing is really, really creepy."

Other former students described Katie as obsessed with being pregnant and having a baby.

At the age of fourteen, Katie allegedly complained to an aunt about her mother's drinking. Worried about Katie and her sisters, the aunt told Katie to contact social services and Cabinet for Families and Children. Allegedly, the Cabinet found and verified the alcohol misuse, but no neglect or abuse. According to Katie's father, this angered Katie and her behavior began to change.

Tim Smith claimed Katie kept insisting she was ill and she constantly begged to be taken to the doctor. Meanwhile, Katie fared poorly in school and had a fistfight coming home once on the school bus. When Tim and Cindy took her to the emergency room, the doctors always informed them that Katie was not sick. The Smiths attempted to obtain psychological help for her, but Katie refused. Katie, her father reports, became a very convincing liar. In another strange incident, Katie reported ghosts haunted her bedroom.

Soon after the ghost incident, Cindy Smith, Katie's mother, overdosed on pills. She survived, but her children were placed with an aunt. The court appointed an attorney as guardian for the children and a court hearing took place to determine the best interests of the children. Tim Smith maintained custody of the children. To monitor the situation, the court assigned a caseworker. Katie soon moved in with her cousin.

In June of 2000, Tim and Cindy Smith voluntarily gave custody to relatives while they sought alcohol treatment. Cindy attended a program in Falmouth, a rural town not far from Independence. Tim Smith, while working as a painter at Paul Brown Stadium, attended an outpatient treatment program at St. Elizabeth Medical Center. He also attended A.A. meetings.

Even so, the children's life had little stability or comfort. However, turmoil and dysfunction had not always been hallmarks for the Smith family.

In the early years of their marriage, when the girls were younger, Tim and Cindy tried to provide a normal life for their daughters, complete with birthday parties, family vacations and camping trips. The family visited Kentucky's array of beautiful state parks, places like Lake Cumberland near the Tennessee border, an idyllic setting known for its lake coves, waterfalls and lush forests.

Trips out of state were also made to Tennessee, North Carolina and Lake Erie, Pennsylvania—all picturesque locales for young girls eager to see different parts of the country.

A Dysfunctional Family

Back home in Kentucky, Tim Smith often whisked the girls away on family fishing trips to a relative's farm in Pendleton County, a large rural community south of the Smith's home in Independence.

However, as time passed, the Tim and Cindy Smith marital union became a troubled relationship. Both developed severe dependency problems, including alcohol abuse which later spiraled. Though they appeared to be in love and have a strong bond early in their marriage, the situation deteriorated over the years. Eventually they divorced.

Many of Tim Smith's problems could be traced to his own sad childhood in Fort Thomas, Kentucky. His father died when Tim was only eleven. Tim's mother overcompensated, catering to him so much that he became petulant and selfish. Even though Tim's mother doted on him and they lived together, he refused to help in the house or even drive her to or from work when she asked. Tim loved to hunt and fish on a farm his brothers owned in nearby Pendleton County, but when it came time to pay his share of the lease, which was only $250, he refused. Relatives described him as lazy and adrift, someone who just seemed to "hang out" and not really have much of a future.

Tim changed for the better, at least for a while, after he met and fell in love with Cindy. Like his mother, Cindy babied Tim. He "worshiped the ground Cindy walked on" according to a friend who knew the couple at the time.

The Smith family followed a suburban migration of sorts to Independence to raise their family.

Relatives remember Katie Smith as a happy, chatty

and vibrant child. Intelligent and articulate, she suffered from either a real or perceived lack of attention that manifested in imagined illnesses and stretching the truth. Once in junior high school and again at Simon Kenton High School, Katie falsely told friends she was pregnant.

Katie told social workers that it was not her, but students at school who began spreading the pregnancy rumors during her eighth grade year. Worn down by the rumors and persistent questions about a possible pregnancy, Katie said she finally lied and told them they were right, she was pregnant. "I just wanted to be left the heck alone," Katie said. "But teachers were asking me all this stuff. For a while I told them I wasn't pregnant. I was like, 'No, no, no, no, no.' Finally, I asked somebody, 'Would it make it better if I just said yes?' And they said, 'Yeah, then we'd know the truth.'"

"I said, 'Yeah, fine, whatever.'" Other times it was reported that Katie faked panic attacks and claimed to have Lupus, a kidney disorder. The family spent thousands of dollars on aqua-therapy and other treatments for Katie's many forged illnesses. Trips to the emergency room, though frequent, rarely if ever resulted in the actual diagnosis or treatment of Katie's problems.

In court papers and media interviews, Katie's father, Tim Smith, said a combination of family problems and his daughter's own demons led her down a path of manipulation.

"Getting attention became an obsession with her," Tim Smith said. "I think it was a self-esteem thing. She felt like she didn't have friends. It was tough on her." Tim Smith admits his own behavior contributed to

Katie's problems and played a role in creating a dysfunctional family.

"My wife and I both drank too much. It progressively got worse. In the later years, when the alcoholism got worse it was kind of dysfunctional. It seems like it impacted Katie the worst."

Her manipulation of the facts, her ability to lie and deceive, eventually emerged as a fatal flaw.

Looking back at fourteen, friends and relatives recount when Katie reported her parents and her behavior began to change after one disturbing incident at home as her parents slowly drifted deeper into chronic alcoholism.

Katie, upset the state investigators found no abuse from her parents' alcohol abuse, began lashing out. Her grades hit bottom.

Tim Smith, who had quit working and did little more than stay home and drink, tried to convince Katie to see a psychiatrist, but she refused.

Smith was convinced Katie's medical problems were "imagined."

"I was the one who took her to the doctor most of the time," he said. "I took her to physical therapy, hydrotherapy, water therapy, and to the hospital for panic attacks. She asked to be taken to the doctor very frequently."

Katie became known to the emergency room doctors, some of whom admitted they knew she was not ill. Instead of "treating" her with medicine—which would have been fruitless since the young girl wasn't actually sick—the ER staff sometimes calmed her down by simply having her breathe into a brown bag.

Court records indicate that relatives attempted to intervene, but to no avail.

Tim's brother said he and his wife remember that when Katie was in junior high she used the pregnancy ruse and went so far as to wear maternity clothes to school.

"Katie told my wife (a former nurse who has worked in the medical profession for thirty years)," her uncle said, " that she has been diagnosed with: Lupus, Crohn's Disease, multi-cystic kidneys, polycystic ovaries, fibromyalgia, degenerative joint disease and gastro esophageal reflux disorder."

"When my wife inquired about the treatment she was undergoing and attempted to discuss these conditions, Katie became very evasive and then changed the subject to yet another illness because none of these conditions proved to be true," he said.

Katie not only resisted seeking psychiatric help, but she became sarcastic at the mention of such treatment.

"I'm just a crazy child," she mockingly told a social worker. "Hey, I'm psychotic. My dad has told me numerous times that I need to go for a psychiatric evaluation. I've said, 'take me. If I am that crazy, just take me.'"

Evidence of the family's problems was rife. One important clue was that the Independence Police found their department no stranger to Tim Smith's house over the years. Their police file on the Katie Smith investigation contains a long history of police "runs" to the residence. A review of them sheds light on the dysfunctional home where Katie grew up. Part of these police reports read:

May 25, 1998 "Physical/Abuse Neglect"
"Responded to above address for a 911 hang up. The victim (Katie Smith) was crying and stated her father had grabbed her and tried to force her to her room. She also stated he slammed her into the wall, the perpetrator denied slamming her into the wall. The other children were extremely upset to the point of hiding in the bathroom, and one child vomited. The house was extremely dirty upstairs and down."

December 14, 1998 "911 Hang Up"

May 29, 1999 "Drug Overdose"
"Female subject was intoxicated (4-5 glasses Jack Daniels) and ingested 11 Rx Naproxen 500 mg. Male subject had a scratch on his right cheek where female scratched him. He stated he had butted her. Both were settled toward each other with the concern focused on the female's status and the two children. Independence Life Squad transported female to hospital because of the pills she took."

July 25, 1999 "Domestic Dispute—Inactive"
"Father, Tim Smith, stated that he and his 16 year old daughter got into a verbal

argument over the use of the phone. The daughter wanted to leave; her mother, Cynthia, attempted to stop her; at this time the daughter pushed her mother down along with her sister who is 12 years old. The younger girl also sustained some minor scratches on her left arm."

August 26, 1999 "Call Complainant"
Dog Bite

October 18, 1999 D.V.C. Case Follow-up Investigation

October 22, 1999 "Wanton Endangerment 2nd Terrace Threatening"
A man filed charges against Tim Smith for shouting at him: "I will fucking have you killed. I know people and I will have you killed."

May 27, 2000 "Well Being Check"
(Cindy Smith reported drunk)
Upon speaking to the children they stated that there are roaches all over the house and that they had lice for a long period of time.
The mother was taken to the hospital for detox by the children's grandparents.

June 6, 2000 "Missing Person"
Cindy and Tim Smith's older daughter reported them missing.

July 29, 2000 "Dispute"

A woman in back yard screaming complaint advised she was crazy.

August 16, 2000   "Warrant—EPO"

September 18, 2000   "Warrant EPO"
                     Search Warrant

October 18, 2000   "General Relay of Info"

October 20, 2000   "General Relay of Info"
                     (Ref Possible Child Abuse)

December 11, 2000 "Chest Pain"

December 12, 2000 "Chest Pain"
                     Tim Smith transported to hospital.

December 21, 2000 "Investigation"

January 21, 2001   "Investigation"

January 25, 2001   "Suicide"
                     Male Subject Suicidal
                     Possibly Intoxicated
                     They Have Been Arguing

February 11, 2001   "Chest Pain"
February 12, 2001   "Chest Pain"

February 17, 2001   "Threatening"

March 19, 2001   "Warrant EPO"

May 26, 2001 "Well Being Check"
          Reference to sex abuse charges causing
          Tim Smith depression.

June 6, 2001 "Chest Pain"

"Tim Smith never worked," said Amy Chapman, an Independence Police detective who investigated allegations of child molestation against him, accusations that were made by his own daughter, Katie.

"He stayed home with the kids," Chapman told the *Kentucky Post* in February 2005. "We were over there all the time. He'd be drunk and come to the door naked. That home was one of the most disgusting and filthiest homes I've ever been in."

Photographs of the Tim Smith house taken by the Independence Police reflected a cesspool of filth. A toilet looked as if it has never been flushed. Stovetops appeared to have never been cleaned. Garbage was piled everywhere, on the floor, in furniture and on the counters. Laundry was dirty and piled and strewn all over. The kitchen table had so much junk on it that it is unusable. The kitchen sink had stacks of dirty dishes. The inside of the house was not inhabitable. No one must have ever cleaned the house. The stench had been unbearable.

"The house in general was just a trash pile," Katie told the Independence Police in March 2001, when they were investigating claims of abuse. "There was garbage on the floor; the whole house was just trash."

A Dysfunctional Family

"My room literally looked like garbage bags had been opened up and just dumped on the floor. There were all kinds of things that weren't even mine. You couldn't walk (on) the floor; you have to move stuff around to make an aisle into the floor."

The woman, who was appointed Katie's guardian after she was removed from her parent's home, described a scene of putrid squalor in the Smith household in September of 2000. She and Katie went to the house to check on the family dog and retrieve some of Katie's belongings.

"We flipped on the kitchen light to see," the woman recalled. "There were dirty dishes everywhere, pots and pans with burned food, overflowing garbage. Stench, bugs, roaches, gnats flying everywhere. Food all over the floor, grease, little pellets of some kind of poisonous material, I wasn't sure what. Pellets on the stove with dried, burnt food; the refrigerator smelled, there was old food in there."

By the time Katie Smith made allegations of abuse against her father, Tim and Cindy had split up. Detective Chapman said Katie took on the role of mother, something she did even before her parents separated.

"Katie, growing up, was the caregiver of that home, taking care of the house, feeding everybody and getting her sisters ready for school because her parents were unable to," Chapman told the *Kentucky Post*. However, judging from the home conditions, Katie failed as a homemaker.

The life of Katie Smith and Sarah Brady share one common thread. Both knew financial struggle.

However, Sarah probably faced more severe financial stress. In addition, Sarah knew displacement and endured multiple moves across the country. She also knew the pain of not having an involved father.

Chapter 21

Striking Similarities, Fateful Differences

Unlike Sarah Brady, Katie Smith had a father involved in her young life. Katie's father, nevertheless, was not always a positive influence. However, the glaring difference in their lives was the love and support Sarah received from her mother and the utter dysfunction in Katie's family. Growing up Sarah at least had the stability of one involved parent and a loving grandparent. Katie had to deal with two alcoholic parents. Despite poverty, Sarah was able to focus on her studies and was not forced to live in a sordid environment. One must wonder if their tragic intersection on the fateful day Katie tried to steal Sarah's unborn fetus would never have happened if Katie Smith knew the love and support Sarah knew.

When she was a young teenager, Katie stated she was disgusted with the situation at home and moved to Ludlow, Kentucky to live with a cousin.

Ludlow is an aging river town which has the feel of a

sleepy little village. It is located a short distance down the Ohio River from Cincinnati. Katie spent her senior year at Ludlow High School, a much smaller school than Simon Kenton, the one she had attended when she lived with her parents, and graduated in 2001. While in school she worked at a small diner where kids gathered after classes for burgers, shakes and ice cream.

Co-workers remember Katie as sweet and friendly, but insecure and an emotionally needy young girl of eighteen. She wanted to be loved and often broke into tears when telling the owners about her family situation, her unhappy childhood and her desire for emotional stability.

They also remember something else about Katie. She appeared obsessed with having a baby. At one point, Katie even began wearing maternity clothes, but no one can ever remember her actually giving birth or coming around later with a baby.

"She was consumed by it," the owner of the diner recalled to WLWT, a Cincinnati television station. "She was always talking about being pregnant."

Around the same time, Katie professed to have a revelation about her past, one she said occurred at a very unusual time—while performing oral sex on a boyfriend.

During that sexual encounter, Katie claimed to see her father's face and, for the first time, allegedly remembered doing the same thing with him. Katie told Amy Chapman, the Independence Police detective, that from about the time she was seven until she was thirteen her dad forced her to perform oral sex on him.

Time to understand and decide on the validity of the

sex abuse allegations helps paint a portrait of the mental state of Katie Smith. Family members were convinced that she used the claims against her father to retaliate against his years of drinking and to have her sisters removed from the family's home so they would not be subject to the same awful conditions she had been.

On the other hand, there was little doubt because of her psychological needs and imbalance that Katie also desperately wanted the attention from the investigation, just as she used phantom medical problems to garner notice.

During Tim Smith's trial on the molestation charges, the prosecutor said Katie had no reason or motivation to make up the charges against her father. According to a letter Smith's brother sent to the Kenton Circuit Judge who heard the case, she had several insentives.

"We believe she had several reasons," he wrote. "Growing up in an alcoholic, dysfunctional family as she has, would certainly cause embarrassment, resentment and absolute hatred. She did not want to see her three younger sisters go through the horror of living in that environment with Tim and Cindy."

"More importantly to this case, however, is Katie told us that she 'would do whatever it took to be sure that her parents never regained custody of her sisters again'," he went on.

After an investigation, police brought molestation charges against Tim Smith. He stood trial in 2001. Katie appeared to be a victim of "repressed memory syndrome," a somewhat controversial diagnosis of a situation where a disturbing memory is stored away in the subconscious and triggered by an event or circumstance. In Katie's case, it was theorized that having oral sex rekindled her "repressed" memory of committing the same act on her father years earlier.

Katie testified during the trial that the alleged sexual abuse started with her dad "soft tickling" her and progressed to him putting his genitals in her mouth. If she didn't perform to her dad's satisfaction, he slapped her behind with a ping pong paddle.

Katie told police that her father's sexual advances and molestation began when she was seven years old and lasted until she was thirteen. "She remembers numerous sexual encounters with her father," according to a police report that was based on an interview with Katie.

Katie said her bad memories included her father fondling her genitalia and penetrating her with his fingers as well as performing oral sex on him, Katie told police.

Katie also reported Tim Smith even had a pet name for Katie when he was preparing to molest her—"Daddy's special girl."

According to Katie some of the sex acts took place when Katie said she was forced to go camping alone with her father.

"She recalls being made to go to bed naked and her father naked nearly all the time," according to the police report. "Ms. Smith stated that her father would sometimes come to her room and other times be called to his room."

Whenever he called, Tim Smith would be naked, Katie told police. If she was dressed "he would pull her pants down and her shirt up and fondle her."

The acts became more brazen and lurid according to Katie. Katie said she was forced to fondle her dad and give him oral sex. She said she can remember him ejaculating at least two or three times.

Katie also reported having disturbing dreams that involved her father taking nude snapshots of her while she slept. She reported the dreams to police in March 2001 during their investigation of Tim Smith.

Katie said she had the dreams while recovering from surgery in which doctors removed her appendix and performed a biopsy on lymph nodes that had been swollen for months.

Somehow the pain, fear, and perhaps the semiconscious state she lingered in was alleged to trigger recollections of other frightening times. "It was completely dark in my room," Katie said in describing the dream to police. "I remember my bedroom door opening and I could see the bathroom light shining into it and my dad was standing in the doorway."

In the dream, Katie's dad was wearing nothing more than a shirt. He sat on her bed, began talking and eventually puts his hand on her leg. She was naked in the dream.

Katie's dad then took her hand and put it on his penis. She tried to pull away but couldn't. Then, he forced her to perform oral sex.

"I just remember him moving my legs around," she said. "And he had a camera."

"He finished, pulled up the blankets and kissed me on the forehead and said, 'Good night special girl'," Katie said.

But was it a dream or was it a brutal reality? Photographs allegedly of Katie's genitalia were eventually seized from the Smith home as part of their investigation, though it was never clear who took the photos. One theory, which she denied, was that Katie, or someone at her request, took the photos.

Though Smith and other family members have vehemently denied the allegation of molestation, at least one relative recalls a troubling situation involving a naked Smith and another one of his daughters.

As part of their investigation Independence Police interviewed Tim Smiths's sister-in-law. She told police that in 1991 Smith and his older daughter had visited their home to go fishing.

When it was time for bed, Smith's sister-in-law expected that Smith's daughter, who was eleven or twelve at the time, would sleep in the same room as her young son.

But Katie's father had other plans. She, Smith said, would sleep with him on a fold out couch in the family room.

"I was like, 'Okay, you know best, you're the dad,'" his sister-in-law said.

She awoke the next morning to find an unsettling scene in the family room.

"When I got up, I could see his jeans lying over by the fireplace," his sister-in-law said. "Then he rolled over and I could clearly see he was completely naked."

The girl, the woman recalled, was dressed.

She thought he even told his daughter to get up and get his pants.

The defense for Tim Smith at his trial tried to

discredit Katie as a witness, citing her history of fabricating illnesses and pregnancy. The girl's mother and three of Tim's other daughters testified that Tim never touched any of the girls sexually. It was the entire family versus Katie.

Tim Smith has also denied he ever molested Katie.

"I didn't do it," Smith told a television reporter. "Never. I never did anything remotely like it."

Oddly, the presumed police officer boyfriend, whose sex act with Katie allegedly rekindled her memories of abuse, wasn't called by either the defense or the prosecution. This boyfriend denied being a boyfriend. However, pictures show them together in what appeared social dating situations. And while the prosecution called an expert witness who testified on the subject of repressed memory syndrome, Tim Smith's attorney did not rebut the testimony with an expert of his own, reportedly because Smith could not afford to pay an expert. The expert called by the prosecution would later prove controversial.

What apparently moved the jury to convict Tim Smith was a picture of the ping pong paddle Katie said her dad used on her behind if she failed to please him. The picture was introduced as evidence by the defense in the trial but never openly discussed in court by either the prosecution or the defense.

Tim Smith, who testified in his own defense, vehemently professed his innocence; he reportedly turned down a plea bargain that would have given him just three years, preferring to take his chances in court rather than admitting any guilt. Smith was convicted of sodomy and sentenced to twenty years in prison.

"Bottom line is I'm in for something I did not do," Smith related in a 2005 jailhouse interview. "You know, I'm not in here charged with being an alcoholic. I'm in here charged on something that I did not do."

"Katie did not want her parents to get the children," her aunt revealed. But the aunt went on, "He was a wonderful father. He loved his daughters. They were the light of his life."

Katie also claimed that her older and younger sisters were molested, but the charges have never been substantiated.

The sisters at trial "both stated that Katie's allegations were not true, but (they) were never given the opportunity to refute them at trial," Tim Smith said in a court filing. "Nor did the jury hear about these allegations at trial."

In the letter to the judge, Smith's brother said that after talking to Katie's sister, they are certain the molestation never occurred.

"Katie's sister certainly has some anger at her parents for her upbringing, but she is absolutely adamant that Tim never sexually abused her or any of her siblings," he wrote. "Had that fact been allowed as testimony, I feel that Tim would have been acquitted on all charges."

Further, the jury was not told "of Katie's history of lying to her teachers, counselors and other health care providers."

Tim Smith also believes his daughter concocted the sex abuse allegations to prevent her parents from ever regaining custody of the children.

Smith's brother harbored no illusions about the type

of parent Tim Smith turned out to be, "not a very good one," he acknowledged to the judge.

"Being the parents of three sons and a daughter ourselves, we are absolutely appalled by my brother's repulsive lifestyle, his laziness and alcoholism," the brother wrote. "He has become a complete failure as a person and provider. There is a tremendous amount of resentment for Tim's neglect of his family. I can only imagine how his children must feel having grown up in that atmosphere."

"Even though Tim Smith was a lousy parent, he would not stoop to the unfathomable level of sexually molesting his own daughters," his brother insisted.

"We are convinced that Tim, though a poor excuse for a parent, could not and did not sexually abuse any of his children," Smith's brother emphatically wrote to the judge. "We would be the first to call for the greatest punishment possible if we thought Tim was guilty; yet we know he is not."

The brother said he and another brother often saw Tim lovingly interacting with his daughters during family outings on the Pendleton County farm.

The girls "were always talking about seeing deer and turkey, roasting marshmallows and camping and hiking with their father," Smith said. "Does that sound like sexually abusing children? For all his faults, Tim does love his children in his own way."

So why then does his brother think Smith was convicted?

He says Tim Smith's background as an alcoholic who was unwilling to work and his scruffy appearance, augmented by long hair, surely didn't score many points with the jury.

"The basic reason is that Tim's poor character, unkempt appearance and details of his family neglect caused the jury to despise him and want to punish him for his past," his brother said. "Sensing the jury's growing dislike for Tim, the prosecuting attorney further appealed to their emotions without proving Tim's innocence beyond a reasonable doubt.

"He asked them to believe the testimony of a young, college bound girl and not to believe the testimony of a deadbeat alcoholic."

For a long time, Tim Smith appealed his conviction to no avail. However, he continued his efforts to prove his innocence. He referred to the pattern of his daughter's lies and the lack of credibility of repressed memory syndrome in his arguments for early release from the Kentucky prison where he was incarcerated.

Chapter 22

The Police Listen and Speak

The Fort Mitchell Police Department investigation involved numerous corroborative reports from third parties related to Katie Smith's "pregnancies" and other misrepresentations.

On February 10, 2005, at the request of Sergeant Bussman, Specialist Shane Best of the Fort Mitchell Police Department walked the neighborhood surrounding Katie Smith's apartment to look for witnesses. A woman approached Officer Best and asked him who was involved in the stabbing. Officer Best explained that Katie Smith was one of the involved parties. When the woman asked how Katie was doing, Officer Best informed her that he did not know. After Officer Best asked the woman how she knew Katie Smith, she explained she did not want to get involved.

Nevertheless, Officer Best engaged the woman in further conversation:

The woman made the comment that Katie was

*married to a Police Officer who worked in the area.
After some prodding, the woman told me the name of
the officer. She then advised that Katie had just given
birth to twins five to six weeks ago and that one of them
had passed away. The lady also thought that the officer
was the father of the twins and that he had been at the
hospital every day prior to the baby's death. The infant
who survived was supposed to be at the hospital. I
asked the woman how she knew Katie, and she stated
that Katie had helped her with her children and that
she and her husband had assisted Katie financially on
several occasions. The woman then explained that she
had to leave so she could visit Katie at the hospital.*

An absolutely remarkable tale! There was only one
individual manipulative enough to concoct such a
story—Katie Smith. The police confirmed that Katie
Smith was not married nor was she involved in a
serious relationship.

Sergeant Tom Loos met with two other young
women who were acquaintances of Katie's on February
10th as well. They had suspicions about Katie's
pregnancies. One said that she attempted to find the
grave of Katie's deceased baby at Spring Grove
Cemetery where Katie claimed the infant was buried.
The cemetery had no record of the child or Katie.

Both girls told Sergeant Loos about a photo album
that Katie carried in her purse with photographs of
Katie pregnant, ultrasound pictures and pictures of
someone else's twins. Then they had an opportunity to
take a close look at the book once and discovered that
the name part of the ultrasound photos had been
"whited out" with correction tape. They were able to

scratch off part of the white out mark and discovered the name underneath. The name indicated the mother of the triplets. Katie babysat the woman's children in her home.

On that same afternoon of Feb. 10, 2005, Amy Krist was at work, overseeing the receptionist desk at a massage therapist's office in Kentucky. Amy answered a phone call expecting to schedule yet another appointment.

However, much to Amy's surprise, the woman on the other end of the line was the legal guardian for Katie Smith. Amy and Katie had known one another for nearly ten years, having met as teenagers while members of the same youth group. But the women were estranged. Katie told too many lies about herself and her life. In the past Katie had claimed to be pregnant, claimed to be the mother of twins, but Amy said the stories never turned out to be true.

"I got sick of her lying to me," Amy said. "I fell for it every time, but I was done with all of that."

Amy had recently married and attended massage therapy school. She was eager to start a new life and Katie was on her mind once in a while but other things occupied her. They had not talked much in recent months. However, Amy began thinking about Katie in early February because she remembered Katie's birthday was arriving soon.

Amy was busy setting up her own home, but she wanted to let Katie know she was still thinking about her. So, she sent Katie a text message.

After all, Amy recalled, the two women had been friends and for quite some time. Katie had often confided in Amy about her personal life, though Amy doubted the veracity of some of Katie's tales and circumstances, particularly when it came to pregnancies and babies.

"I really didn't want to talk to her," Amy said. "But I wanted her to know that I wished her well so I texted, 'Happy Early Birthday' because it was a day before her birthday."

Katie didn't respond. Amy figured she had gone out to have some drinks. Katie liked to go to bars and she liked to drink, even when she was pregnant. Amy recalled just a few months earlier when Katie had gotten so drunk at the Beer Cellar, a Newport, Kentucky bar that sits atop a barge moored along the Ohio River and directly across from downtown Cincinnati.

It was shortly after that drunken night in the riverfront bar that Amy stopped hanging out with Katie. But that happened months before in the winter; Amy wondered why Katie's guardian was calling now.

The woman started telling Amy that Katie had pretended to be a pregnant woman named Sarah Brody. The woman asked Amy if she knew Sarah; she did not.

"Then she just basically told me," Amy said about the jolting phone call. 'I knew you and Katie had a falling out, and I just wanted you to know she's dead'. I was shocked, I couldn't believe it."

The woman only knew a few details, but a television in the massage therapist waiting room was turned on, and before long the story of Katie's death was on the news.

"It was just so weird that this happened and Katie was involved," Amy said. "How can you do that? How can you steal a baby from someone? I didn't think Katie had any idea how to do something like that, to take a baby out of woman's stomach. But I guess she tried."

Amy said she realized over the years that Katie had a problem telling the truth, though when Katie made accusa-tions against her father, Amy did believe the allegations that Katie made.

"Her dad was always very cold," Amy said. "I know he might be innocent and eventually get out of jail, but I had believed her allegations about her dad."

But Amy insisted she never had an indication that Katie could do something as violent as attacking a pregnant woman with a knife and then taking the woman's baby.

"I never felt afraid in any way when I was with Katie, never," she said. "So when I heard what happened, it just blew me away. Katie lied so much; I knew she was a compulsive liar, but I never thought she was a bad person.

"But she was mentally ill, more so than I ever knew."

Amy began to flash back to her relationship with Katie and piece together telltale signs. Katie and Amy had met in 1996 when both were members of Job's Daughters, a youth group that performed community service in northern Kentucky. Amy was sixteen, Katie just thirteen.

"When I was younger, I was kind of caught up in my own world and didn't care too much about what other people were up to," Amy admits at this point. "I was kind of selfish."

So when Katie said that she had gotten pregnant but had a miscarriage, Amy was not really interested, because she was too wrapped up in herself, as are many teenagers.

"I didn't know what to say when she told me that story. I was like, 'whatever, you're fine now, let's talk about what is happening now.'"

Despite their age difference, Amy and Katie spent time together. Amy could drive and she often invited Katie to hang out together. Katie probably reveled in the attention from an older girl. The two were friends but, because of their separate interests and age difference, they didn't have the kind of strong intense relationship many young girls establish during their teenage years.

A few years later when Amy was planning to marry for the first time in 2002, she asked Katie to be a bridesmaid in the wedding. Katie had gone away to college after graduating from Ludlow High School, but had told Amy she was eight months pregnant and couldn't be in the ceremony.

Later, when Amy confronted Katie about the pregnancy, Katie said that she had had a Caesarean section, but the baby had been still born.

"I didn't want to talk about it," Amy remembers. "At the time I didn't even want to have kids."

After Amy's marriage the women didn't see much of each other. However, Amy's marriage did not work out and she divorced in 2004. In the spring of that year Katie remerged in her life.

"I had a new apartment in Kentucky, and she came over," Amy said. "She told me though she wasn't close to the father, she had gotten pregnant and had twins. I was a bit more mature at the time, and I took some interest in what she had to tell me. I told her she had to talk to the father about what they were going to do."

Katie told Amy that the baby's father did not believe he had gotten Katie pregnant. He was demanding a paternity test to establish if he was the father of the babies.

"Katie told me the father said that if it turned out the babies were his, he wanted to give up his paternal rights," Amy said.

Amy thought it strange that Katie was always alone whenever the two women got together. Katie said that the children were staying with her aunt and uncle. It was the same excuse Katie used every time Amy asked to see the children. They were always with some relatives.

Except one time when Amy was at the Bellevue Veterans Club, a neighborhood bar and community gathering place near the Ohio River in northern Kentucky. Katie called Amy's cell phone and told her to come out to the parking lot.

"I got out to the parking lot, and Katie was sitting in a van with twins in car seats in there with her," Amy said. "I knew she didn't own a van, but I didn't ask. I was interested in meeting the twins, because it was the first time I had ever seen them."

Knowing what she knows now, Amy figures Katie was just watching someone else's kids as part of one of her baby-sitting jobs.

"I realize just how much I didn't know about what was really going on," she said. "I knew she was lying about some things, but I just sort of blew it off. I never really put two and two together."

In the late summer and early fall of 2005 Katie once again claimed to be pregnant. Though this time Katie said she didn't want the baby.

"She already had twins, supposedly, so I told her to put the baby up for adoption, because there are plenty of people out there who can't have kids and desperately want to become parents."

At this point in Katie's friendship with her, Amy had noticed a change in Katie. She was going out more often, drinking and sitting in smoky bars even though she said she was pregnant.

"I was thinking that maybe this time she was for real about the pregnancy," Amy said. "But she would go out, hang in bars and drink too many shots."

Katie's favorite cocktail was called a Red Headed Slut, a mix of peach schnapps, Jagermeister herbal liqueur and cranberry juice. Katie was drinking those drinks one night when she became inebriated at a Newport bar and needed Amy's help.

"She was so drunk we had to carry her up to her car, drive her home to her apartment in Fort Mitchell and then carry her up the steps," Amy said.

Amy found something that night that disturbed her. On the floor of Katie's car was a knife. Amy was thinking, *what the hell is that doing in there?* while she stared at the sharp glistening silver edge.

That night Amy said she made a decision, "I decided not to talk to Katie any more. I knew she wasn't telling me the truth about what was really happening, about things going on in her life. But she wouldn't let go."

Katie was persistent and continued to call Amy sometimes after midnight and later. The messages were similar if not verbatim: I'll give you the answers to everything if you call me back.

Amy eventually gave in and returned a few of Katie's phone calls. Katie rambled on and on. She often talked about men but offered no viable explanations about some of the lies from the past.

"I'll give her credit for one thing; she always kept her stories straight," Amy said. "But it's sad because she was living a lie."

When Amy was interviewed by the police investigating Katie's death she told them she had no idea what Katie had been planning. "I had been in her apartment, but I never saw anything like the medical equipment they say they found in there."

Amy went to Katie's funeral. Katie's family was there. There were even some of the girls from the Job's Daughters group.

"It was on Valentine's Day," Amy said. "I went because we had been friends and because I really wanted some closure with the whole thing."

Amy became pregnant that May. She had always been partial to the name Katelyn, but decided not to give her daughter that name because of the date she was born: February 9th, the same day as Katie Smith's birthday.

Only two days after the birth of Amy's daughter on February 11, 2005, Specialist Hyett spoke to a woman for whom Katie Smith babysat. Katie was hired through an agency to assist with the woman's twin babies born in December of 2003. Katie started working around February 2004. The agency advised the woman that Katie was in nursing school and was working in

Behavioral Health Department at St. Elizabeth Medical Center. She was let go after eight weeks due to lack of mental stability.

On that same day, Sergeant Tom Loos interviewed a woman who is the mother of twins born at the end of September 2005. The woman Katie worked for previously referred Katie Smith to a family with young children, because she knew the family was searching for a nanny. The mother employed Smith as a nighttime nanny for her twins from the beginning of October until Thanksgiving. Katie watched the twins Sunday through Thursday. Her employment was only temporary, because Katie was supposedly expecting twins herself and would only be able to work until the arrival of her babies.

Katie told the family that she was married. Katie claimed she and her husband were high school sweethearts. He was a police officer. She wore a wedding ring. According to Katie, they split up because he fathered a child with a dispatcher. As Katie explained it later, after the arrival of Katie's twins they began to reconcile. She asserted that her husband was spending a lot of time at the hospital with the surviving twin.

The woman said that Katie's employment ended before Thanksgiving. Katie called her employer one evening and announced that her water had broken. When the woman arrived home, there was a visible puddle on the floor. Katie said she had been placed on bed rest and was unable to continue working. She said she was going to see her doctor. Later she called to say she had delivered twins by Cesarean Section in January.

LEFT: Sarah with her sisters and mother.

ABOVE: Sarah and her sister Carolyn on vacation at the bottom of Mount Ranier in Washington State.

LEFT: Sarah in her high school cheerleading uniform.

ABOVE: A young Katie Smith during an earlier period in her life.

ABOVE: Katie Smith at home in her apartment.

LEFT: Katie Smith at a children's clothing store during one of her faked pregnancies.

ABOVE: Katie Smith's apartment building, scene of the crime.

ABOVE: After the attack: blood covered y mat.

RIGHT: Katie's extensive collection of baby clothing and bys that she accumulated in preparation for her planned etal kidnapping.

ABOVE: A baby's bedroom set up in Katie Smith's apartment.

RIGHT: Katie's deflated pregnancy suit cast off at the scene of the crime.

LEFT: Katie stocked up on baby formula and all the necessitites for a newborn infant.

ABOVE: Katie Smith displaying her faked pregnancy.

BELOW: Katie assembling a child's high chair in preparation for the baby of her anticipated kidnapping.

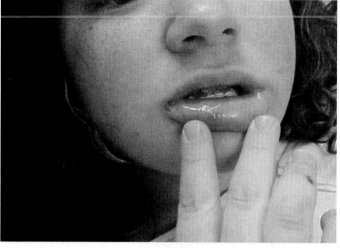

ABOVE: Sarah Brady showing the cuts on her lip from her savage fight with Katie Smith.

RIGHT: Sarah displaying several defensive wounds on her hand and cuts beneath her fingernails.

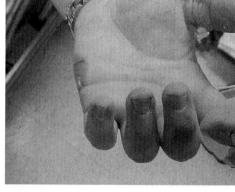

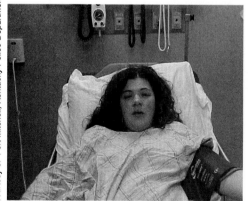

LEFT: Sarah recovering in the hospital after Katie Smith's attack.

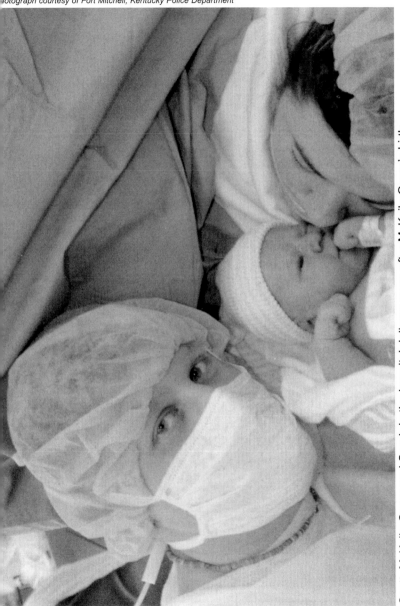

Scott, McKaila Grace and Sarah in the hospital delivery room after McKaila Grace's birth.

ABOVE: Scott holding his newborn daughter, McKaila Grace.

RIGHT: Scott's son holding his little sister, McKaila Grace.

ABOVE: Sarah and McKaila Grace near her first birthday.

The employer thought it very strange, because she knew it was not possible for Katie's pregnancy to continue for several weeks after her water broke.

But Smith continued her fantasy. In fact, it became more involved. Katie said that she delivered at University Hospital and that one of the twins was transferred to Children's Hospital with heart problems and later died. The other she supposedly named 'Brennen' lived but was also admitted to Children's Hospital with stomach problems.

The Sunday before her attack on Sarah Brady, Katie called her former employer and left a message on her machine. The woman did not call her back.

Also on February 11th, Officer Roy Taylor from the Fort Mitchell Police received and reported a call from a caseworker at Young Families of Children, Incorporated regarding her former client, Katie Smith. The caseworker reported that Katie enrolled with Young Families of Children, Incorporated for assistance on two occasions, once in November 2003 and again in November 2004. In both instances, the agency assigned Katie Smith a caseworker. Apparently, a second caseworker for Family Services of Northern Kentucky was also assigned to Katie Smith. Remarkably, the original caseworker reported that she believed Katie Smith not only gave birth to twins in December 2003, but one was stillborn and the other child died from an aneurysm. She even related that the second caseworker attended the funeral. She also reported that one of Katie Smith's caseworkers from Young Families was told by Katie that her due date was December 21, 2004, then changed it to January 9, 2005 and finally to February 5, 2005. The original caseworker stated that Katie Smith planned to be induced on February 11, 2005 after receiving her prenatal care at University of Cincinnati Hospital. This information supported Katie's timing on her attack on Sarah Brady.

The Fort Mitchell Police obtained information that the twin babies names were Olivia and Isabella. Officer Taylor phoned Spring Grove Cemetery, the alleged burial place of the twins, and spoke to the front desk receptionist. At Officer Taylor's request, the receptionist searched the internet records for Olivia and Isabella by a first name search then a last name search of Smith. After checking the records, including section twenty-seven, the infant section, from 2001 to present, the receptionist failed to locate any records for Olivia and Isabella.

Officer Taylor, of the Fort Mitchell Police Department, also spoke with a woman regarding an alleged auto accident involving Katie Smith on October 15, 2004. The woman reported Katie suffered from chronic back pain before the accident and back pain after the accident. The woman recalls Katie wore maternity pants.

Soon after the attack while at the apartment scene, Sergeant Bussman met Katie's landlady. She informed Sergeant Bussman that her family owned the apartment complex which was the crime scene. The woman informed Sergeant Bussman that Katie Smith was a tenant. She inquired whether Katie had gone into labor. The landlady then took Sergeant Bussman on a tour of Katie's apartment. She pointed out that Katie lived on the first floor, another tenant lived on the second floor, and a third tenant lived in a makeshift apartment in the attic. Sergeant Bussman noticed that there weren't any apartment numbers attached to any of the doors, and he didn't receive a response when he knocked on them.

Previously in 2003, Katie worked as a Certified Nursing Assistant for the Saint Elizabeth Medical Center. Fabrications were suspected after Katie's third reported pregnancy. She was referred for a fitness for duty evaluation at the St. Elizabeth Employee Assistance Program.

With regard to Katie's medical "conditions," one psychologist commented that Katie suffered from "serious psychological and behavioral problems" and that "her depression is frequently manifested in physical ailments."

The same psychologist noted that Katie "has resorted to fabrication in an attempt to gain attention from others" and that Katie has "an intense desire to care for young children, which improves her sense of self-worth." The psychologist concluded that Katie's patients could be at risk and given Katie's "apparent preoccupation with having a child and caring for children, we recommend that she refrain from engaging in any work-related activity that places her in a position of responsibility for children..."

According to at least one family member, the fourth time Katie alleged pregnancy, it lasted about eleven months, ending with Katie's death. Katie had explained that she was past her due date and she was supposed to be induced within days of her death. She told a number of people that she was due on different dates at various hospitals. This is consistent with Katie's history of creating what amounts to basically untraceable stories.

More facts about Katie's early life begin to reveal themselves when Katie's former junior high school teacher discloses intriguing elements of Katie's past.

Ruth Roberson told the story of how she'd been shocked when she found out eighth-grader Katie Smith was pregnant.

Katie was in Roberson's eighth grade pre-algebra math class at Kenton County's Twenhofel Middle School, a large public school where students from both the suburbs and the country attended.

The teacher recalled Smith as being an average student, a nice kid with lots of friends, but no steady boyfriend.

"That's what really shocked me when I heard she was pregnant," Roberson said. "Katie didn't really have a boyfriend. I would see her with other girls, but not with boys. I didn't think she was seeing anyone. She was nice, but she was heavyset."

Smith certainly didn't try to hide her pregnancy. Katie's former teacher states that though Katie was still a child, she seemed quite proud and excited to become a mother.

In most cases, the pregnancy of a young girl Katie's age was met with shock, outrage, anger, sadness and sympathy. Society can be harsh and judgmental. People instantly assign a Scarlet A to a girl for carelessly engaging in unprotected sex when barely a teenager.

However, Katie and her friends appeared to be embracing the pregnancy, eager to participate in the impending birth. Ruth felt Katie wallowed in the attention.

Roberson said, "She brought books and catalogs of baby clothes and baby items into school. Katie and the other girls were planning a baby shower. Katie's friends were excited, talking about who was going to be the godmother, planning to hold the shower at school, picking out baby clothes."

According to her former teacher, Katie seemed remarkably calm. Her life was about to drastically change, the stigma of a baby being born out of wedlock was hanging over her head and the responsibility of a raising a child was about to be thrust upon her at a young and immature stage of her life.

"She was obsessed with babies," Roberson said.

According to Katie, she was in the early stages of pregnancy but she wasn't yet showing signs of carrying a child. Katie's teacher and a different teacher decided on an intervention. They took Katie aside and asked if her parents knew about the baby.

Smith told her teachers that her parents were unaware of the situation.

"We told her," Ruth Roberson said, "either you talk to your parents or we will."

Tim Smith was enraged after hearing about Katie's pregnancy from her teachers. He was livid and in denial.

"He blasted me on the phone," Ruth said. "He was screaming, yelling at me, asking me why I was telling tales about his daughter. He let me have it. He insisted that his daughter wasn't pregnant. He was furious at me because he assumed that I was making up the story."

Mr. Smith insisted, "Katie wasn't that type. She wasn't pregnant."

Roberson, who had dealt with irate parents during her years working at a junior high school, didn't argue with Smith. She listened to his angry remarks, realized he didn't want to admit what she believed was the obvious and asked him to put Katie on the phone.

Ruth asked Katie, "Why haven't you told your parents that you are pregnant?"

"She said she didn't know why she hadn't told them," the teacher said. "She really didn't appear to have an answer."

Other teachers, Katie's friends, kids at school and most certainly the parents of other students were aware of Katie's alleged pregnancy.

"Everyone just assumed it was all true," the teacher said.

Of course it was untrue, and was the first of many elaborate pregnancy ruses Katie would stage throughout her life. She continued to live in this bizarre fantasy world until the day she attacked Sarah Brady.

Roberson eventually received a call from Katie's mother. She was much calmer than Katie's father and was clearly interested and concerned with what had been going on.

"She had very specific questions; she asked if Katie mentioned going to a doctor, and if she had received blood tests. Mrs. Smith seemed interested in other details of the pregnancy," Katie's teacher said.

It was during the conversation with Mrs. Smith when Katie's former teacher discovered that Katie's eighteen-year-old sister was pregnant and going through everything Katie had been talking about: doctor visits, picking out clothes, planning a shower.

"It was at that moment that I realized Katie had been making the entire thing up," Roberson said. "She was imitating her sister. She was living through her sister."

Katie's teacher couldn't believe what she was hearing. Katie had been very convincing. The story that it was now known she had fabricated was intricately fashioned and she seemed sincere and truthful. The young girl deceived her closest friends and her teachers.

"I should have realized at the time," Ruth said, "that there were to be more problems down the road."

The teacher also found out that when Katie was at home she had spent a great deal of time looking after and babysitting her one-year-old sister.

Katie was the middle child among her two sisters. Because the eighteen year old was pregnant and the young one still a toddler, both sisters were receiving more attention. Katie couldn't make herself a small child again, so instead she pretended to be pregnant to garner notice from her family and friends.

Having spent a career in classrooms and sometimes having dealt with the occasional troubled child, Smith's teacher knew that counseling was available for Katie and her entire family. She suggested therapy as a beneficial option for Katie.

"You can suggest getting some help, which is what I did," Roberson said. "Sometimes they take the advice, sometimes they don't."

Roberson did not directly confront Katie about the pregnancy. The school year ended and Katie moved on to high school. During that time her junior high teacher saw her once in the halls at Simon Kenton High School.

"She came up, hugged me and told me everything was okay, everything worked out."

About a year later, Ruth Roberson heard from Katie. The letter reassured the teacher that Katie was coping with her problems in accepting reality.

"I'm writing to tell you how sorry I am for hurting you this past year. I had no excuse to do that to either one of you. Things in my life now are still confusing. I feel so horribly for hurting you guys in that way. You were kind and sweet. All you were doing was caring. I took advantage of you and I can't ever forgive myself for that. It was wrong. I am so grateful for both of you. I really hope that one day my life will be back in order so I can put all of this behind me. But until then, and most likely after, I will never forget you two. I will always be thankful. Love always, Katie Smith."

The teacher never heard from Smith again.

Of course she did hear shocking revelations about Katie, just as many others did, as she sat watching the evening news on the night of February 10, 2005, the day Katie died while trying to steal Sarah Brady's unborn child.

"My jaw dropped open when I saw the news," Roberson said. "I just couldn't believe it."

Ruth Roberson quickly called the other teacher who had also participated in Katie's intervention. She had to tell her what happened.

The other teacher, who had also been watching the news, was at the same moment trying to phone her colleague.

"We were just shocked, and we had a weird feeling, because our first thought was that Katie had been lying about this pregnancy," Roberson said. "We knew, because we had seen her do it before."

The teacher was also aware that Katie could be a convincing and manipulative liar since she had known Katie during her earlier fabrications.

"That's what made the news even more shocking," the teacher said. "I never thought Katie was the kind of kid who would commit a crime. She was never in trouble. She was a nice person."

Having lived through Katie's earlier pretense of pregnancy, the junior high teacher understands how Sarah Brady had been lured to the Fort Mitchell apartment that day.

However, having been sympathetic to the troubled young girl, Katie's previous teacher struggles with trying to understand Katie's motivation for her bizarre and ultimately deadly betrayals.

Roberson stated, "I don't know if Katie really wanted a baby or if she craved the attention that is associated with a child. In one way the attack surprised me, but at the same time someone should have seen this coming."

On February 17, 2005, Sergeant Tom Loos spoke with a woman who employed Katie as a childcare provider. The woman is the mother of nineteen-month-old twins who hired Katie Smith to watch her children during the first part of August 2004. Katie continued watching her children twice a week until the fourth of October.

The previous employer said Katie was recommended by another mother, and said she pursued Katie for the nanny position. Katie came to the woman's house and interviewed with the woman and her mother. Katie smelled of cigarette smoke and the woman asked if she was a smoker. Katie told her that she wasn't. The woman was slightly concerned about the possibility of deception, but hired her anyway because she was desperate. Katie never presented herself as pregnant to the family she worked for.

Katie claimed to have recently moved into a rent-to-own house with her fiancé, and said they were trying to have a baby.

One morning, Katie called to say her fiancé had been in a very serious car wreck. She alleged that the night before he had driven to a bar and picked up a drunken friend. He was driving home and while attempting to cross the I-471 Bridge, he was cut off by a tractor-trailer that stopped abruptly in front of him. He was able to stop his car, but was struck by the vehicle behind him and slammed into the truck. According to Katie, her fiancé suffered two broken femurs, a broken collarbone, and a back injury. Later, he was transferred to Drake Hospital for rehabilitation. Katie emotionally told the woman she'd worked for that her fiancé did not have disability insurance and the lack of his income during the recovery period was causing them financial hardship.

According to her employer, one day Katie showed up at the house of the family for whom she was employed with two baby seats in her car. Katie was never allowed to take the twins she watched anywhere in a car. The mother of the children asked Katie why she had baby seats with her. Smith told the woman that the seats were intended for other children she watched.

Not long afterward, Katie asked for permission to take the twins to another family's home for a pre-arranged visit. The woman refused permission. Later, she discovered that no arrangements had been made with the other family.

As the police interviews continued, more and more bizarre stories about Katie Smith emerged.

Chapter 23

More Strange Reports

On February 17, 2005, Sergeant Tom Loos received an anonymous call to the police department from a man claiming to be a former Simon Kenton student who attended classes with Katie Smith. He said that Katie had often made statements about being pregnant over a two year period during their sophomore and junior years. He stated that she often complained about not feeling well because of her pregnancy. The former student also remembered Katie warning classmates not to pick on her because she was pregnant. Although she said these things over a period of time that would encompass two pregnancies, she never became visibly pregnant. He wasn't in the least bit surprised when he heard the news accounts of the events surrounding her death.

On February 18, when Detective Nottingham met with Katie's prior employer and her husband, they compared ultrasound pictures collected during the search of Katie's apartment with their own. No definite matches were found, although they were missing some of theirs and could not be certain that they were not among those collected.

The family who employed Katie provided copies of cancelled checks, references given by Katie prior to her employment, and two pages of a calendar with notations indicating the days Katie was to watch the family's children.

A teacher from Twenhofel Middle School remembered Katie Smith from her years as an adolescent. She called Gary Kaiser from the Kenton County Police Department. At one point in time, Katie told anyone who would lend an ear that she was pregnant. The school was concerned about the issue and contacted her father regarding the situation. According to school officials the father discounted the information.

.On a later date, the family who previously employed Katie met with Sergeant Tom Loos and Detective Scott Nottingham at the Fort Mitchell City Building in response to a request for a meeting. They both spoke about their experiences with Katie and discussed the information Katie shared with them regarding her background.

A different family had hired Katie as a "cuddler" for twins. The position was temporary and she stopped working for them once the twins began sleeping through the night.

The woman then hired Smith at her office to transcribe medical reports. After a short time, Katie stopped showing up for work. When her employer inquired, Katie claimed that she was unable to come to that location. The employer provided Katie with a computer and dictaphone so that she could continue to transcribe the reports at home. Katie never returned or finished transcriptions. Some time later, Katie returned the dictaphone. The computer was never returned. The employer identified the computer removed from Katie's apartment as the one she loaned her.

The woman and Katie stayed in contact. The former employer described her relationship with Katie as a close and ongoing friendship. She felt sorry for Katie who seemed to suffer one tragedy after another. Because Katie's stories included constant financial hardship, the woman gave Katie gifts of money on occasions.

Katie's previous employer produced birth certificates, photographs from the delivery room, and ultrasound photographs of her own twins.

Each of Katie's employers added strange but relevant elements to the portrait being drawn about Katie in the months preceding her attack on Sarah Brady.

On February 22, 2005, Police Specialist Scott Nealy met with an acquaintance of Katie's at the Fort Mitchell Police Department. The woman came in voluntarily for an interview.

The woman said that she had known Katie Smith for around nine years. They met when Katie was thirteen years old. She said she and Katie were best friends when they were young teenagers. The former friend said that she was aware of at least four pregnancies that Katie had claimed over the years.

This woman added another strange recollection of Katie's fabricated past. She spoke of the first story she'd heard from Katie having occurred at the age of thirteen. It was then Katie revealed to her friend that she had a miscarriage.

The second pregnancy Katie told her about occurred in April of 2002 when Katie was attending Midway College. She said that the baby was delivered during an emergency C-section and was stillborn.

The third pregnancy allegedly occurred in January of 2004. Katie's friend gave Katie a baby shower. Afterward, Katie created a story of one of her twins being stillborn. The other infant, according to Katie, was born with serious medical problems and remained in the hospital. Katie's friend asked Katie how the sick baby was feeling and wanted to know when she could see it. There was always an excuse about where the baby was and who was caring for her. Katie told her friend that the father of the twins was a former police officer.

After three claimed pregnancies, Katie still was able to live this lie only one last time. On this occasion, she alleged the father was someone else. Katie's friend said the last time she spoke with Katie was in December of 2004. At that point, the friend realized Katie lived in a fantasy world. She could no longer deal with Katie's lies. As a result, she cut off all ties of friendship with Katie.

Katie's friend also mentioned that Katie was involved in an accident on Fort Washington Way in Cincinnati in 2004. Katie was taken to the hospital and told doctors that she was pregnant. When Katie's friend arrived at the hospital to be with Katie, the doctor came into the room to do a pelvic exam and Katie asked her friend to leave. Katie's friend inquired about the baby, but Katie wouldn't answer any of the questions.

The friend told the police that they needed to also talk to another girl who was friends with Katie shortly prior to Katie's death. Katie's friend said that the other woman became very close with Katie around October or November of 2004.

Scott Nealy also met with one of Katie's former boyfriends at the Fort Mitchell Police Department on February 22, 2005. Katie's previous boyfriend came in voluntarily for an interview.

He explained that he was a chemical engineer.

Katie's ex-boyfriend said a woman asked him to dinner and brought Katie Smith with her. This took place in September of 2004. Katie's former boyfriend and Katie dated a couple of times and he said they had sexual relations in September and in October. Katie called him a couple of times after October and he told her he didn't want to date her anymore. She continued to call him even though he was no longer interested in pursuing a relationship with her.

According to the ex-boyfriend, in December of 2004 Katie showed up at his apartment and told him she was pregnant. He said they went to a drugstore and bought a pregnancy test kit. They took the test back to his apartment and tried it twice. Both tests came back negative. A couple of weeks later, Katie called him and told him she went to the doctor and the pregnancy test was positive. Katie's previous boyfriend said they discussed the matter and he urged her to get an abortion. They made an appointment at a clinic in Cincinnati and went in to fill out the medical forms. Right before the date, Katie called him and said she wasn't going to go through with the abortion and planned to have the baby. He told her that was fine, but he wanted a paternity test to prove it was his child. He also claimed that she stopped by his apartment and showed him two ultrasound pictures she claimed to be of her baby. He said the pictures she showed him had the name cut off at the top of the page. He asked her why the name was not on there and she told him that the photo machine cut it off. He told police the last time Katie's ex-boyfriend spoke with her was the week before Christmas of 2004.

Katie's previous boyfriend also said when he was dating Katie she claimed to have twins with another man. Katie's ex-boyfriend went to her house and she told him the father had the babies. He never saw the twins or photographs of the twins.

On November 28, 2005, Detective Scott Nottingham spoke with a relation of Katie Smith who, as it turned out, was Sarah Brady's teacher and cheerleading coach.

The teacher/coach met Sarah when she was a student in her eighth grade English class. She then coached Sarah's cheerleading squad for all four years of Sarah's high school. She also had contact with Sarah at school rallies, special events and as a class sponsor. Following high school, the teacher had contact with Sarah at least four times a year until Sarah became pregnant.

The teacher described Sarah as being a good

student who never lied, made good decisions, was quiet and passive. It was very hard to tell when Sarah was angry and she never witnessed anger or aggression from Sarah. According to the teacher, "When Sarah became upset, she cried and talked about the problem." As Sarah matured through high school, Sarah became more confident and spoke her mind.

The teacher could only remember hearing about one confrontation that Sarah had during her high school years. That involved a fight with another girl over Sarah's boyfriend, Scott. She remembered being surprised because Sarah had always been a mediator, preventing confrontations from becoming physical.

The teacher further stated that Sarah's post high school years demonstrated her dedication as a parent to Scott's son and that she was always pleasant to be around.

On December 13, 2005, Detective Scott Nottingham spoke with a young woman who met Sarah Brady in 1997 when they worked together at a bank. They continued to work together until December 2004. In addition to being co-workers, they became friends and spent time together socially.

From December 2004 until then, the teacher stated that she had contact that usually involved lunch with Sarah about once a week.

She described Sarah as being trusting and too nice. She stated, "Sarah was never emotional and would become quiet when upset." Sarah's co-worker said the only other way to tell if something was bothering Sarah was through her facial expressions.

Her colleague did make the observation that Sarah

.was very jealous of Scott and he was jealous of her. When asked about any problems that this caused, the woman said that it may have resulted in a disagreement between them but she was unaware of anything more than that.

After learning various bits of Sarah Brady's high school years and Katie Smith's disconceritng past, Detective Scott Nottingham spoke with Timothy M. Smith, Katie's father, at the jail where he was incarcerated on February 2, 2006. Trying to learn more about Katie's personality, the telephone interview had been previously arranged with the cooperation of Warden John Motley. This interview occurred as a result of Mr. Smith claiming that he had information that would be relevant to the police investigation of Katie Smith and Sarah Brady.

When asked directly, Mr. Smith admitted he had no information for the police and had no recommendations of who should be contacted to further the investigation.

Tim Smith did express interest in learning of the investigation and getting information that would be useful with his upcoming appeal. He was told that he would be able to learn of the investigation once it was closed and it became part of the public record. He was also informed that the purpose of the call was not to discuss his appeal and that he should address those issues with his attorney.

On February 10, 2006, Detective Nottingham spoke with Katie's Smith's former roommate at Midway College.

Her previous roommate said Katie told her that she was pregnant at the age of thirteen. According to Katie, a classmate was the father and the baby allegedly died at birth.

Katie also spoke of being pregnant in 2001 while attending college. Despite the fact that Katie's roommate was her best friend, she never accompanied Katie on any medical visits. Katie always went to the doctor's office alone. During the winter school break, the roommate went to Florida with Katie. In 2002, she left Midway College and a short time later, Katie told her that baby 'Aubrey' was stillborn and was buried at the hospital's graveyard. Katie's friend could not recall the name of the hospital, but did remember it was located in Lexington. Katie then moved in with her friend and stayed with her for six months before returning to northern Kentucky.

In 2003, Katie told her friend that she was pregnant again, and this time she was carrying twins. Katie's friend later learned that the twin girls were born, and were named 'Olivia' and 'Isabella'. The friend believed that the twins actually existed until Katie's death.

On a rainy day in March of 2004, Katie's friend met with Katie, but the twins weren't with her. When she asked about the children, Katie told her that she didn't want to bring the twins out due to the bad weather.

Later that same year, Katie told her friend that she was pregnant yet again. It seemed as though Katie had been pregnant for about a year. Katie told her friend that pregnancy actually lasts ten months. She said she was due to give birth on December 2, 2004. Katie's friend learned that she was scheduled to have surgery on December 22, and apparently heard from friends that Katie had told them that she was due the same day.

The strange bits of news about Katie Smith's past grew more puzzling with each new revelation. The line between truth and fantasy blurred.

Chapter 24

The Whole Truth

Given Katie Smith's history of making up stories, why did the jurors and others think her father guilty based on her testimony about his abuse? And do they still feel the same way? One person who may have had a change of heart is the foreman on the jury that convicted Smith.

The juror, although it is surprising the defense allowed him, was a former police officer who left law enforcement to work as a professional diver. He did not find Katie totally credible on the stand. However, he said jurors were swayed by the ping pong paddle photograph.

"A photo the defense introduced showing a room in the house had a ping pong paddle in it," the foreman said. The jury logic went like this. Katie said there was a paddle. There is a paddle in the photo. Therefore, she must be telling the truth. Of course, there are flaws in this logic. Simply because there is a paddle, it doesn't mean

Katie performed oral sex on her father.

Another juror interviewed in October 2005 believes that knowing about Katie's lies with the Sarah Brady incident, he would have probably voted to acquit Tim Smith. Of course, the jury had already heard an abundance of evidence relative to Katie lying and faking, but at the time of the verdict obviously chose not to believe it.

There is a principle in the law that sometimes a case must be over for better or worse. The logic and public policy is that there must be finality. Yet, if you happen to be the one on the "short end of the stick," such a maxim seems questionable. Truth and justice, justice and law, should, but do not always meet.

When asked, the defense attorney for Tim Smith stated he never knew the foreman of the jury was a police officer. The parties to trials, through their attorneys, in Kenton County, receive jury fact sheets prior to jury selection which name their occupation. Police officers are not kept on juries in criminal cases by any defense attorney. Police officers are more than likely going to be sympathetic to the prosecutors who they work with versus the defense attorneys they often see as spin doctors.

Had the defense never called Tim Smith, the foreman of the jury believes the jury would have acquitted rather than convicted. Upon learning more about Katie's pattern of telling lies after the trial, the foreman had even more doubt about Smith's guilt.

However, Jonathan Stoudmire, a forensic psychiatrist at University Hospital in Cincinnati, said Katie's proclivity to lie could very well be a sign that the abuse occurred.

"To me, it sounds like factitious disorder," Stoudmire told The *Kentucky Post* in 2005.

"People who suffer from factitious disorder get something from taking the role of a sick person," he said. "Being pregnant is almost like that. You get a lot of attention when you're pregnant. People with these types of disorders often have something traumatic happen to them when they were younger. If she was indeed molested by her father, that relationship was shot and she had a huge void in her life."

With her father headed off to prison, Katie set out to obtain what she wanted most out of a life—a baby.

After one of Katie's allegations, the Independence Police Department opened an investigation. Allegedly, Katie never remembered the abuse until one day while having oral sex with her "police officer" boyfriend; she "saw" her father's face and "remembered" she had oral sex with her father.

"An act with a boyfriend triggered memories of my father doing the same type of things. When I first started having sex with (the boyfriend), I saw my father's face," Katie said in a social worker's report. "I just recall doing the same thing for my father, oral sex."

Later in 2000, after Katie Smith made an allegation of sexual molestation against her father, the Court revoked the visitation rights of Tim Smith. After another hearing, the court determined there was no abuse and Tim Smith's visitation rights were reinstated. Despite Katie's allegation, the fact that her two sisters denied any abuse by their father was indicative of Katie's tendency toward compulsive lying.

The social worker asked Katie how her father would respond to the allegations of molestation.

"There are all kinds of things," she said. "I'm like a path-ological liar. I'm crazy in the head, too. I'm nuts." Imagine. She admitted she was a pathological liar and then becomes the chief witness in the criminal case.

And the theory of repressed memory syndrome is very controversial. Although it has been used to substantiate some cases of abuse, some of these have later proved false.

A specialist on false and repressed memory, has worked on high profile court cases that include Martha Stewart, Michael Jackson and Oklahoma City bomber Timothy McVeigh. She told one television reporter that Katie's testimony was inconsistent and that testimony given by the prosecution's expert witness on repressed memory syndrome was flawed.

"There is no credible, scientific support for this notion," the specialist said. "What's being claimed here are years and years of molestation, triggered supposedly by somebody touching her head during some sexual involvement when she had other sexual experiences before and there never were any triggers of these years of molestation."

She went on to say, "It just raises a red flag."

Katie's story about performing oral sex on her father changed over time, the authority found in her review of the case.

She points to what Katie told social workers in July 2000, when she said she "put her mouth" on her father's penis "a couple of times." The authority on repressed memory syndrome compared that statement to what Katie said in September 2001: "Probably more than ten times, but not like 6,000 or anything like that."

"If this therapist, who testified at Tim Smith's trial, had bothered to go back and look at the interview that had occurred more than a year earlier, the therapist would have seen that it wasn't so consistent," the repressed memory syndrome specialist told the station. "It was that combination of testimony that contributed to (Smith's) conviction."

In the appeal of his conviction, Tim Smith took a similar approach in trying to cast doubt on Katie's reliance on repressed memory.

"We believe that a substantial possibility exists that the result (of the trial) would have been different without the repressed memory syndrome testimony," Smith claimed.

For state crimes in Kentucky which rise to a felony level, the prosecutor is called the Commonwealth Attorney. When Tim Smith was prosecuted for sexual abuse charges against Katie Smith, the Assistant Kenton County Commonwealth Attorney, John Osterhage, called the State's expert witness. John Osterhage, a part-time prosecutor who looks like John F. Kennedy with a mustache, is an honest and solid prosecutor. He is not a prosecutor interested in putting someone behind bars who may be innocent.

The State's witness theorized that Katie suppressed her father's abuse. Other evidence at trial were items obtained by Katie Smith and her cousin when they broke into Tim Smith's house. The friend claimed she found Polaroid photos of female genitalia in Katie's bedroom inside a cookie jar. Also in the cookie jar were pages from a pornographic magazine. A police warrant found other sexual materials in Katie's room, but Tim Smith denied ownership. The jury did find Tim Smith not guilty of use of a minor in a sexual performance. This appears to be what is called an inconsistent verdict. How could they believe there was sex, but not a "sexual performance?"

The photos taken from the home of Tim Smith depicted something more than pornography. The police seized not only photographs of naked woman taken by a Polaroid camera, but also videotapes. Many of these photos were of entirely naked women, not Katie. Also included were Polaroids allegedly of Katie Smith's genital area. These photos did not show a face. The police believed they identified that Katie's scar was the result of a surgical procedure. However, they may not be of Katie or maybe they were of Katie, but who took them and when? Katie "found" them with her cousin, so there is a cloud of suspicion.

Katie's cousin told Independence police that on September 17, 2000, she and Katie visited her parent's home. Tim and Cindy Smith were reportedly in a rehab facility in Florida; their daughters were in the care of state appointed custodians. Katie wanted the opportunity to retrieve some personal belongings, including some figurines, from the house. She also wanted to check on Fred, the family dog.

No one was home when the girls arrived. They entered through an unlocked rear door. The house was filthy. Dirty dishes were piled everywhere. Bugs scurried across the floor and flew through the air. The whole house had a stench.

Katie and her cousin tossed some clothes for Katie's younger sisters into a laundry basket. They walked into Katie's room. Katie's cousin described it as a disaster area.

"You can't even walk around in her room," her cousin said. "There are piles of plates, rotted food, and dirty clothes. You could not step into her room . . . to even put your toe in without stepping on something."

In addition, Katie's cousin recalls seeing a grotesque scene throughout the room.

"There were dead bugs everywhere, in every drawer," she said.

Katie collected her figurines and clothes. The girls filled two boxes and a bag. Then, just as the girls were preparing to leave, Katie's cousin made a curious discovery.

Tucked away in the corner of a closet was a ceramic cookie jar fashioned in the likeness of a strawberry. Because the jar did not have a lid Katie's cousin could see something was stuffed inside.

Katie's cousin picked up the jar and asked Katie if it belonged to her.

"No," Katie told her, "I've never seen that before."

According to later reports, Katie's cousin began pulling the contents out of the jar and recognized immediately that it contained sexually oriented material. Upon seeing what was inside, Katie's cousin first froze and then threw up her hands and began "running around," repeatedly asking, "What is that? What is that?"

"I don't know," Katie's cousin replied to the frantic Katie, "there's some porn stuff in here."

The Independence police report indicates the jar contained "various items of a bizarre and inappropriate nature." Those included used condoms, undeveloped film, vaginal cream and part of a pregnancy test kit. According to court documents also found in the cookie jar were a pornographic magazine, herbal soap, a baby bottle, tissues, an empty pack of menthol cigarettes, tampons and a pencil.

But the most troubling items in the jar were six photographs of a naked woman with only her stomach and genitalia showing.

"You can't see hands," Katie's cousin said. "You can't see anything but the private areas."

When Katie's cousin showed the photos to Katie, she supposedly ran from the room screaming and crying. Her cousin caught up with her and tried to calm Katie down.

"I don't know what those are," a hysterical Katie told her cousin. "Those weren't there before. I don't know who that belongs to and I don't know why it's in my room."

Katie's cousin convinced Katie to look at the snapshots, but only after agreeing to cover up the most intimate parts. Katie's cousin knew that Katie had stretch marks and unique scarring from some previous health problems. The girl in the photos had similar marks.

Staring at the photos, Katie looked at her cousin and said, "That's me, that's me."

Tim Smith's brother pointed out in his letter to the court that the photographs came up during Smith's molestation trial.

"Katie's credibility came into question with her testimony concerning the pictures," Tim's brother said. "She indicated that the photos were taken while she was in a drugged state after exploratory surgery on her abdomen, which, as it turned out, was unnecessary."

"Her sister testified that she had seen Katie with her Polaroid camera and the pictures prior to when Katie testified that Tim took them," he said.

Tim's brother said while the jury convicted his brother on sodomy charges, they acquitted him on charges related to the photographs.

"The jury apparently felt, as we did, that if Tim had taken the pictures he wouldn't leave them in a cookie jar in Katie's room for anyone who came in to see," Smith said.

Did Katie take the pictures herself and plant the snapshots in a jar to implicate her father? Or did her father really take them? No one will ever know for certain.

As days passed, Tim Smith, from his prison cell at the Eastern Kentucky Correctional Complex in Richmond, Kentucky, claimed he was an alcoholic, but never a sex abuser towards Katie or any of his other daughters. Though the prosecutor offered Tim Smith a plea bargain which included a three-year prison sentence, he still continued to maintain he would rather do hard time knowing he is not guilty. Smith says he would never admit to something he didn't do. After the first trial, he was scheduled for parole in 2021 with no chance of early release unless he admitted to the sex crime.

"I wasn't guilty and I wasn't gonna say I was," Smith told a television reporter during a jailhouse interview in

March of 2005. "Not gonna do that. I said from day one it never happened and it never happened. And if I have to spend twenty years in here, I will never say that I did it when I didn't."

One of Katie's cousins claims Katie Smith testified against her father to remove him from the house, because she didn't want to be forced to babysit under threat of her father. Tim Smith's appeals failed based upon what is called "failure to preserve the issues for appeal."

In Smith's cell, he kept pictures of his family, including a snapshot of Katie and two of his daughters from a long ago family vacation in North Carolina.

"What do you think when you look at these photos?" the reporter asked Smith.

"It's sad."

"You look like a happy family," the reporter observed.

"We were," the father replied.

Smith told the reporter he found out about his daughter's death during a phone call from his brother.

"I didn't know what to think," he said. "I was amazed, really. I mean, I knew she had problems, but I didn't think she, you know, was capable of something like that."

The reporter asked Smith if a part of him felt sorry for Katie.

"Well, of course. All of me, not just a part, feels sorry."

On July 28, 2005, an attorney from Chicago, Patrick Lamb, filed court papers to aid Tim Smith's attempt to renew his fight for freedom. The attorney was working pro bono. The events of Katie's lies relative to the Sarah Brady incident certainly prompted the action. Part of the argument being made by Tim Smith's new counsel was that Smith had ineffective counsel in challenging the expert who testified against him. The defense attorney had admitted he made mistakes and wanted to help in the cause.

"Tim Smith is innocent," Lamb said in a statement posted on the Internet Web site of his law firm. "He was the victim of his own lawyer's failures, an expert witness for the State who misrepresented herself, and of bad science in the claim of 'repressed memory.'"

The expert who testified against Smith received a doctorate from a university, which Kentucky does not recognize for qualifying to testify as an expert. However, in this trial she did. Unfortunately for Tim Smith, her testimony of "repressed memory" helped put Tim Smith in prison.

"Even though Kentucky law prohibits people who receive degrees from unaccredited universities from using titles such as 'doctor,' prosecutor Jack Osterhage repeatedly referred to the expert as 'doctor' and she, herself, used the title," Lamb said.

"There can be little doubt that testimony from an expert who is a 'doctor' is given greater weight than testimony from someone who is not a doctor," he said. "She should not have been referred to as 'doctor,' and the fact that she was acknowledged by the title, severely prejudiced Mr. Smith."

Lamb also argues that Smith's defense lawyer should have requested a hearing away from the presence of the jury "to determine whether the theory of repressed memory had enough support in the scientific community to be considered reliable enough for the jury to hear the evidence."

In the *Diagnostic and Statistical Manual of Mental Disorders 4th Edition*, popularly named DSM-IV, the American Psychiatric Association's "Bible," repressed memory syndrome is spoken of as dissociative amnesia.

The Austrian physician, Sigmund Freud, revolutionized ideas on how the mind functions and how to treat conditions of the mind. Freud fathered the notion of repressed memory. He suggested it occurred when a patient intentionally seeks to forget an experience, or forcibly repudiates, inhibits and suppresses memory. Freud believed this repression occurs in those victimized by sexual abuse.

Jacqueline Hough, in a 1996 article in *The Southern California Law Review*, expressed and reemphasized the theory:

It is often beneficial for victims to forget these events, because at the time of the abuse a victim experiences a variety of overwhelming emotions including helplessness, fear, shame, guilt, pain and betrayal. To survive, the victim is forced to mentally cope with these emotions because the victim often cannot physically escape the abusive environment. Blurring of the trauma, denial, repression and amnesia of the experience are common ways children cope with the trauma and the accompanying emotions.

The DSM IV describes dissociative amnesia as such:

The essential feature of Dissociative Amnesia is an inability to recall important personal information, usually of a traumatic or stressful nature, that is too extensive to be explained by normal forgetfulness (Criterion A). This disorder involves a reversible memory impairment in which memories of personal experience cannot be retrieved in a verbal form (or, if temporarily retrieved, cannot be wholly retained in consciousness). The dis-turbance does not occur exclusively during the course of Dissociative Identity Disorder, Dissociative Fugue, Posttraumatic Stress Disorder, Acute Stress Disorder, or Somatization Disorder and is not due to the direct physiological effects of a substance or a neurological or other general medical condition (Criterion B). The symptoms must cause clinically significant distress or impairment in social, occupational, or other important areas of functioning (Criterion C).

Dissociative Amnesia most commonly presents as a retrospectively reported gap or series of gaps in recall for aspects of the individual's life history. These gaps are usually related to traumatic or extremely stressful events. Some individuals may have amnesia for episodes of self-mutilation, violent outbursts, or suicide attempts. Less commonly, Dissociative Amnesia presents as a florid episode with sudden onset. This acute form is more likely to occur during wartime or in response to a natural disaster.

Several types of memory disturbances have been described in the explanation of Dissociative

Amnesia. In *localized amnesia,* the individual fails to recall events that occurred during a circumscribed period of time, usually the first few hours following a profoundly disturbing event (e.g., the uninjured survivor of a car accident in which a family member has been killed may not be able to recall anything that happened from the time of the accident until 2 days later). In *selective amnesia,* the person can recall some, but not all, of the events during a circumscribed period of time (e.g., a combat veteran can recall only some parts of a series of violent combat experiences). Three other types of amnesia— generalized, continuous, and systematized—are less common. In *generalized amnesia,* failure of recall encompasses the person's entire life. Individuals with this rare disorder usually present to the police, to emergency rooms, or to general hospital consultation-liaison services. *Continuous amnesia* is defined as the inability to recall events subsequent to a specific time up to and including the present. *Systematized amnesia* is loss of memory for certain categories of information, such as all memories relating to one's family or to a particular person. Individuals who exhibit these latter three types of Dissociative Amnesia may ultimately be diagnosed as having a more complex form of Dissociative Disorder (e.g., Dissociative Identity Disorder).

Many in the psychiatric field claim repressed memories don't exist. Opponents refer to them as "false memories" and insist repressed traumatic memories are all bunk.

Recently, in the nationwide cases against the Catholic Church as a result of the pedophile priests, many victims refered to repressed memory syndrome. The only place in the entire United States where a court certified claims against a Catholic Diocese as a class action is northern Kentucky in Boone County. To prove the unreliability of the repressed memory syndrome, Eric Deters, the attorney co-author of this book, was approached by a friend who asked if they could file a lawsuit because they had been molested as a youth and never did anything about it. The statute of limitations of one year had long expired. This person explained they could claim memory repression. It was clear there was no memory repression. The person never forgot the event. The individual also knew to claim memory repression to attempt to fight the statute of limitations.

In Freud's theory of "repression" the mind automatically banishes traumatic events from memory to prevent over-whelming anxiety. Freud further theorized that repressed memories cause "neurosis" which could be cured if the memories were made conscious. As proponents point out, to this day, Freud's repression theory has never been verified by rigorous scientific proof. However, there may have been other valid psychiatric conditions affecting Katie Smith's mental stability.

The other psychiatric issue present in this case is the question as to why a woman would ever want to make the effort to steal a baby from the womb of a mother. The obvious answer is the person must be mentally disturbed. The effort involved of faking a pregnancy is difficult enough. However, when you add the medical problem of removing the child from the womb in a successful extraction it is hugely difficult as well as bizarre.

Repressed memory syndrome is one topic subject to continued debate. There is also the issue whether or not Tim Smith ever molested his daughter, Katie. His failure to be a solid father, his alcoholism, and his problems with domestic violence left him subject to a false claim, if it was, due to his own credibility issues.

"Mr. Smith was originally convicted based on a theory that does not have support among scientists who have studied the human memory," Lamb said. "The failure to ask for a hearing was profound. In fact, the Kentucky Supreme Court said that the outcome of Mr. Smith's case most likely would have been different if the repressed memory evidence had been excluded."

In an interview with The *Kentucky Post*, John Osterhage defended his actions at Smith's trial.

"It was a well-tried case," he said. "We had the evidence. I have no qualms."

However, in light of the Sarah Brady incident, even John Osterhage has doubts as to Katie's credibility. He also recalls that at the end of the trial, while the jury deliberated, he and Tim Smith were in the courtroom while others were taking their break. Each sat at their respective tables. Tim Smith leaned over and said, "Mr. Osterhage, I just want you to know that I never did this." John Osterhage claims no defendant ever made such a comment before to him in all the years he prosecuted.

Patrick Lamb made Katie's Smith behavior a central part of his appeal of Tim Smith's conviction.

"Katie Smith's bizarre behavior prior to her death is compelling evidence of her ability to lie convincingly," Lamb said. "Katie Smith had convinced family members and close friends that she was nine months pregnant at the time of her death."

"Her pregnancy was faked," he wrote. "Anticipating claims that her bizarre behavior is somehow evidence of having been molested, the appeal includes affidavits from leading therapists, (including Dr. Harrison G. Pope Jr. of Harvard Medical School), that the diagnosis of abuse cannot be made from any pattern of behavior."

An authority on child abuse explained that if Katie was in fact abused, it may have been a factor in the young woman wanting to have a child even if she had to kill for it.

"This kind of reactional, false pregnancy is very uncommon," states Dr. Carl Adler, a professor of psychiatry at The University of Cincinnati. "But it is true that in some cases the need to be pregnant, the need to have a child can be overwhelming and it can lead to acts of desperation."

As stated earlier, even before her newest plan as she lived at the Kentucky apartment, Katie Smith left a trail of stories regarding pregnancies. At least one psychologist has publicly commented to news accounts of Katie Smith's story that child sexual abuse could be a causative factor in a woman's overwhelming desire to have a baby. Though not married, Katie Smith carried around an ultrasound picture of someone else's unborn twins. Katie also once told family members she had given birth, but the babies died. At another apartment in the Wallace Woods subdivision in the city of Covington, Katie left the impression on at least one neighbor she was pregnant. He told a local television station: "When she left here, she was pregnant enough that she was showing. When we moved in, there was a baby seat in the hallway and a couple of books about parenting and baby care."

Katie apparently told numerous family members the expectant birth date, but kept moving it forward. The last day she told family members was February tenth or eleventh. These dates coincide with her attack on Sarah Brady.

Karen Tinsley, an assistant professor of psychology at Guilford College in North Carolina, reported that it is not uncommon for stalkers to have suffered at the hands of an abuser.

Tinsley writes, "A lot of times stalkers, or serial killers, have been sexually abused in their past childhood, and throughout their childhood they do not develop a conscience like normal people would, causing them to think the evil they are committing is not wrong."

Katie Smith never possessed any medical or surgical training or experience. The "infant replacement" desire of Katie Smith is quite simply beyond bizarre.

The Journal of Forensic Sciences published a study on kidnapping by Caesarean section. It is asserted that those who committed such crimes were self-centered, obsessed with babies, and intended to live in a fantasy world, but were not considered psychotic. As they concoct their brutal plans, they often fail to think ahead to the commonplace questions they'll be asked about suddenly having a child or about practical matters such as birth certificates.

Chapter 25

Smith Fights Conviction

Patrick Lamb made compelling arguments to Judge Patricia Summe of the Kenton Circuit Court to overturn Tim Smith's conviction. The lawyer maintained that the issues involved in the case were complex and not properly pursued. He also felt that the case involved both the scientific validity of the so-called "Repressed Memory Syndrome" and lacked a necessary Daubert hearing. (*Daubert v. Merrill Dow Pharmaceuticals Inc.*, 509 U.S. 579 (1993.) A Daubert hearing is used by the court to determine if scientific evidence is reliable. It is conducted outside the presence of the jury. Lamb cited the Kentucky Supreme Court ruling on the Tim Smith matter: "Here, from a consideration of the whole case, we believe that a substantial possibility exists that the result would have been different without the Repressed Memory Syndrome testimony." Lamb indicated the fact that in Rule 11.42 Motion, substantial scientific evidence proved that there weren't any signs of

Repressed Memory Syndrome and there wasn't scientific evidence to support the claimed syndrome. The list of evidence which Lamb brought out needed to be developed based on the expressed positions and statements is long:

- "It is not known how to distinguish, with complete accuracy, memories based on true events from those derived from other sources." American Psychiatric Association, Statement on memories of Sexual Abuse, 1993.
- "The AMA considers recovered memories of childhood sexual abuse to be of uncertain authenticity, which should be subject to external verification." American Medical Association, Council on Scientific Affairs, Memories of Childhood Sexual Abuse, 1994.
- "The available scientific and clinical evidence does not allow accurate, inaccurate, and fabricated memories to be distinguished in the absence of independent corroboration." Australian Psychological Society, Guidelines Relating to the Reporting of Recovered memories, 1994.
- "At present there are no scientifically valid criteria that would generally permit the reliable differentiation of true recovered memories of sexual abuse from pseudomemories." Michigan Psychological Association, Recovered Memories of Sexual Abuse: MPA Position Paper, 1995.
- "At this point it is impossible, without other corroborative evidence, to distinguish a true memory from a false one." American Psychological Association, Questions and Answers about Memories

of Childhood Abuse, 1995.

- "Psychologists acknowledge a definite conclusion that a memory is based on objective reality is not possible unless there is incontrovertible corroborating evidence." Canadian Psychological Association, Position Statement on Adult Recovered Memories of Childhood Sexual Abuse, 1996.

- "The use of recovered memories is fraught with problems of potential misapplication." American Medical Association, Council on Scientific Affairs, Memories of Childhood Sexual Abuse, 1994.

- "There is no single set of symptoms which automatically indicates that a person was a victim of childhood abuse. There have been media reports of therapists who state that people (particularly women) with a particular set of problems or symptoms must have been victims of childhood sexual abuse. There is no scientific evidence that supports this conclusion." American Psychological Association, Questions and Answers about Memories of Childhood Abuse, 1995.

- "Psychologists recognize that there is no constellation of symptoms which is diagnostic of child sexual abuse." (Canadian Psychological Association, Position Statement of Adult Memories of Childhood Sexual Abuse, 1996.)

- "Previous sexual abuse in the absence of memories of these events cannot be diagnosed through a checklist of symptoms." (Royal College of Psychiatrists, reported Recovered Memories of Child Sexual Abuse, 1997.)

- "The AMA considers recovered memories of childhood sexual abuse to be of uncertain authenticity, which should be subject to external verification." (American

Medical Association, 1994.)

In addition to the memory issue, Lamb argued that there were significant topics which required investigation and could not be conducted by Tim Smith. Pending questions remained in regards to whether or not credentials were improperly exaggerated. Patrick Lamb noted the fact that Katie Smith had an uncanny ability to deceive. Because of his speculations, Lamb required an attorney to conduct on behalf of Tim Smith.

Lamb also possessed experience with repressed memory experts.

Patrick Lamb is a partner with the Chicago law firm of Butler, Rubin Saltarelli & Boyd LLP. Lamb has been practicing law in the state of Illinois since 1982. Lamb also practiced in the United States District Courts for the Northern District of Illinois, the Central Division of Illinois, and the Southern District of Illinois, the United States Court of Appeal for the Fourth, Seventh and Eleventh Circuits, and The United States Supreme Court. Judge Summe allowed Lamb to practice law in Kentucky on the Tim Smith case on what is called a pro hac vice motion. This means he's allowed to practice law only on the one case.

The motion was originally filed by Tim Smith; Patrick Lamb allowed him to receive a Rule 11.42 motion. Motion in the legal business simply means a request. The number of the motion is simply the number of the rule in the rule book. Lamb argued that motion RCr 11.42 authorizes relief when there is a violation of a constitutional right, a lack of jurisdiction, a violation of a statute regarding judgment void and subject to collateral attack and cited this Kentucky case, *Tipton v. Commonwealth*, 376 S.W.2d 290 (Ky. 1964).

Tim Smith alleged his lawyer hadn't told him of his rights nor according to Smith had he been made aware of protections under the law. Smith's lawyer didn't ask for a *Daubert* hearing concerning repressed memory syndrome, object to the testimony of the Commonwealth's expert, take into consideration the credibility of Katie Smith, object to any part of the Commonwealth expert's testimony or her qualifications, object to the prosecution's closing argument, or investigate the identity of the boyfriend in order to test the credibility of Katie's story as to how the repressed memories arose.

Smith said his original lawyer failed to effectively assist Smith, so these objections were not preserved for appeal. Although some objections were heard in his brief to the Court of Appeals, the Kentucky Supreme Court refused to make a determination concerning the issues. There is a rule which requires an attorney to make a record he is objecting to in order for the lawyer to complain about it later. Smith's earlier lawyer failed to do this for Smith.

Tim Smith requested Judge Summe vacate his conviction, because it was constitutionally invalid. Specifically, he alleged he was denied the effective assistance of counsel as guaranteed by the Sixth and Fourteenth Amendments to the United States Constitution and Sections Seven and Eleven of the Kentucky Constitution. Patrick Lamb, on Tim Smith's behalf, specifically alleged these grounds for relief:

- The trial counsel failed to investigate the qualifications of the expert witness used by the Commonwealth to support the scientific foundation for the victim's claim of "recovered memory." Had such an investigation been conducted, trial counsel would have learned that the expert had materially misrepresented her credentials.

- Had trial counsel investigated the qualifications of the Commonwealth's expert, trial counsel would have been able to object to the prosecutor's use of the title "Doctor" to enhance the witness' credibility. The witness repeatedly violated Kentucky law by referring to herself as "Doctor" and the prosecutor aided, abetted and facilitated these violations of the law to enhance Ms. Wolfe's credibility with the jury.

- Trial counsel failed to conduct a reasonable and professionally competent investigation into the "recovered memory" theory about which the Commonwealth expert testified. Trial counsel relied on information supplied to him by the Commonwealth expert, who obviously had an overwhelming incentive not to provide trial counsel the volumes of scientific information that establish that there is no such thing as "repressed memory." As a result, trial counsel was not able to confront the Commonwealth expert with the scores of studies that repudiated the theory she advanced.

- Trial counsel failed to request a *Daubert* hearing in order to challenge the legal sufficiency of the evidence for "repressed memory." The likelihood that the "repressed memory" evidence would have been excluded is high. The Kentucky Supreme Court acknowledged that "from a consideration of the whole case, we believe that a substantial possibility exists that the result would have been different without the repressed memory syndrome testimony." *Smith v. Commonwealth of Kentucky*, 2004 WL 535975, (Ky. 2004).

- Trial counsel failed to challenge the qualifications of the Commonwealth expert to testify regarding repressed memory. The sole extent of her qualifications on this critical scientific theory was the response to a single question about whether she was an expert on repressed memory and her conclusory assertion that she was. To the contrary, there is no indication that the Commonwealth expert is conversant with the scientific literature on repressed memory: it is certain that she has not contributed to it. Her position as a therapist puts her in a particularly vulnerable position testifying in regards to the scientific issue. While as a therapist, she hears people tell stories, she is never in a position to verify the trust of the claimed recalled memory. Thus, all she can do is say that she believes patients who claim to have recovered memories. There can be no approach to this critical issue that is less scientific. This is critical in light of *Stringer v. Commonwealth*, 956 S.W. 883 (Ky. 1977) and the Supreme Court's discussion of this issue in Mr. Smith's appeal.

- Trial counsel failed to object to the substantial body of the Commonwealth expert's testimony that was designed to allow her to testify that she believed Katie Smith's version of events, including specific testimony that the Commonwealth expert found her "credible and believable." The Kentucky Supreme Court has overturned numerous convictions in which experts have sought to bolster the credibility of the victim in this fashion.

· Trial counsel failed to adequately investigate Katie Smith's story that she recalled the memory of her father's sexual abuse while having oral sex with her boyfriend. On information and belief, the purported boyfriend has denied having a sexual relationship with Katie Smith. The importance of such testimony in undermining Katie Smith's credibility is obvious, as is the importance of examining Katie's alleged ex-boyfriend before trial. Trial counsel's efforts to find this individual before trial were lacking.

· Trial counsel failed to adequately prepare for his examination of Katie Smith. The entire case rested upon Ms. Smith's credibility, making impeachment of her with documents critical. Trial counsel did not have documents regarding her physical and mental health that would have impeached Katie Smith on several key points, including her claim that she was diagnosed with post-traumatic stress disorder. Trial counsel's failure in this regard was so acute that the Court admonished him during trial for his failure to have such documents.

· While trial counsel's strategy of avoiding any reference to the Smith's family's prior dealings with Kentucky social service agencies and Tim and Cindy Smith's drinking problems is debatable, his failure to adapt once that evidence was admitted reflects a grossly ineffective defense of Mr. Smith. The very evidence trial counsel hoped would not come before the jury actually was evidence of Katie Smith's motive for fabricating her story. The absence of such a motive was a fundamental underpinning for Ms. Wolfe's conclusions about Katie Smith's veracity, and trial counsel's failure to challenge Ms. Wolfe with this evidence was damning.

Patrick Lamb argued that if any of these claims were true, Tim Smith was entitled to relief under RCr 11.42, which really meant the overturning of his conviction.

Patrick Lamb further argued to Judge Summe that the claims were not clearly contradicted by the record, and as a result, an evidentiary hearing was required.

Marguarite-Neill Thomas and Melanie Lowe from the Department of Public Advocacy assisted Patrick Lamb is asserting the arguments on Tim Smith's behalf to Judge Summe.

Jack Osterhage, the prosecutor involved in Tim Smith's conviction, argued the position for the state.

He struck this blow: "First, that the circumstances involving the death of his daughter and primary prosecuting witness, Katie Smith, are so bizarre and entangled with apparent lies and deceit in 2005 that she must have been equally untrustworthy with her sworn testimony to this jury in 2002."

"Second, that his duly licensed and retained counsel was ineffective in his dealings with the Commonwealth witness, that the result of the jury's verdict ought to be discarded. In effect, the result from that request—in light of the death of the Commonwealth's primary witness—would be the end of this case."

Osterhage continued by stating that the standard of review for Judge Summe required Tim Smith show that his previous lawyer's performance was deficient. His burden required showing that Smith's former lawyer made errors so serious he was not functioning as the "counsel" guaranteed by the Sixth Amendment. Second, Jack argued, Smith must show that the deficient performance prejudiced his case. The burden required showing counsel's errors were so serious as to deprive Smith of a fair trial. An unfair trial meant one whose result is unreliable.

In order to establish prejudice, Osterhage argued, Tim Smith needed to show there is a reasonable probability, but for his counsel's unprofessional errors, the result of the trial would have been different. Reasonable probability had been defined as a probability sufficient to undermine the outcome.

Under Kentucky law, there has always been a strong presumption that the conduct of counsel is within the wide range of reasonable professional assistance. This is so because hindsight is always perfect.

Stating that Judge Summe must be highly deferential in reviewing defense counsel's performance, Osterhage said the judge should avoid second guessing counsel's actions based on hindsight.

Tim Smith was not automatically entitled to an evidentiary hearing on a criminal rule 11.42 motion unless there was an issue of fact which cannot be determined on the face of the record.

Smith's own attorney signed an affidavit conceding his own ineffectiveness. Jack Osterhage argued it was unethical for counsel to assert his own ineffectiveness for a variety of reasons. He cited a Kentucky Bar Association Ethics Opinion.

Osterhage pointed out that the Kentucky Supreme Court rejected the opportunity to hold that admittance of the Commonwealth expert's testimony which was not objected at trial. The fact that the testimony wasn't objected to was so egregious that it constituted palpable error requiring it to address the potential wrong even though not preserved for review.

Tim Smith also challenged his trial counsel's permitting the Commonwealth expert to identify herself as a doctor in addition to her credentials involving repressed memory syndrome. Osterhage argued that a review of the Commonwealth expert's trial testimony of September 6, 2001 from 11:30 A.M. until 12:15 P.M. proves that she was completely honest in her testimony and she was fully cross examined on the issues of which movant now so vocally complains. At 11:27 A.M. she holds a Ph.D. in Psychology. During cross at 12:05:26, she pointed out that her license is in Advanced Nursing. From high noon until 12:15 P.M. an aggressive question and answer exchange takes place regarding repressed memory syndrome and its scientific underpinnings, including discussions regarding movant's post-trial expert contra position on this issue.

Going on to highlight Tim Smith's own Motion for Judgment of Acquittal filed with the Court on September 12, 2001, Osterhage conceded the cross examination of the Commonwealth expert included discussion regarding "debate" in the psychological profession in relation to the existence of repressed memory and, in particular, the accuracy of the memories once recovered.

Then, Osterhage pointed out that at the conclusion of the Commonwealth expert's testimony, she left the jury with the statement you "can't say for sure that anybody's memory is completely accurate."

A weary Osterhage concluded his arguments with one last plea: "Certainly, hindsight is 20/20. As in any case, a retrial would result in a better presentation of the evidence from both perspectives of defense and prosecution. And while the facts surrounding the death of Katie Smith are those which give one pause, they cannot be the basis for the legal conclusion that movant's underlying trial was so unfair or so flawed as to require reversal."

On March 29, 2005, Judge Patricia Summe, who sat as the judge in Tim Smith's trial, issued her Order. She sustained Tim Smith's 11.42 Motion : "During the trial, prior to the presentation of the testimony of the expert witness for the Commonwealth, the Court ruled that the expert would not be allowed to testify regarding the ultimate issue of the honesty of the prosecuting witness. However, during the direct examination of the expert, counsel for defendant failed to object when the expert was questioned as to that truthfulness and when she did testify directly to that issue."

"Furthermore, defense counsel failed to secure an expert of his own or to present any evidence to counter the expert testimony of the witness for the Commonwealth, merely stating in his closing argument that other experts disagree with the theory. The evidence in this case was primarily testimonial, with some pictorial evidence regarding an instrument of persuasion, a ping-pong paddle, which the jury relied upon to base its determination of credibility. While it is not necessary in every case for defense to hire a rebuttal expert, under the circumstances of this case and considering the record as a whole, allowing the expert testimony presented by the Commonwealth to go virtually unchallenged is, under the totality of these circumstances, to be outside the range of acceptable trial tactics. Such failure has been held to constitute ineffective assistance of counsel. *Thompson v. Commonwealth*, Ky., 177 S. W. 3d 782 (2005)."

"The Supreme Court also noted that some of the Commonwealth's Attorney's statements in closing arguments were improper, but that there wasn't any contemporaneous objection thereto by attorney for the defense and, therefore, that Court could not address that unpreserved error."

"In reviewing the record, the Court finds numerous errors committed by attorney for defendant which, taken together, are sufficient to overcome the presumption in favor of counsel and support a finding that defendant was denied the effective assistance of counsel as guaranteed by the Constitution. As a whole, the conduct of counsel in this case falls outside the range of competent legal assistance. This Court agrees with the Supreme Court that there is a substantial possibility that the result of the trial would have been different had counsel provided a more effective defense."

"It is therefore, ordered that the motion of the defendant is granted. The judgment and sentence entered in this case on November 30, 2001 is vacated.

The case shall be returned to the active docket of his Court for a new trial."

In a remarkable twist, Tim Smith won a major victory. His conviction was overturned. He faced another trial or an appeal from Judge Summe's ruling. However, the witness who helped convict him, his own daughter Katie, was dead. She couldn't testify. It's ironic that her credibility was shattered after the fact. The same woman who convicted him freed him from his grave.

Tim Smith was by then fifty-one years old and had already served five years at the Eastern Kentucky Correctional Complex in West Liberty, Kentucky. WLWT-TV in Cincinnati interviewed Tim Smith after Judge Summe's Order overturned his conviction:

A saddened but philosophical Tim Smith commented: "There's a light at the end of the tunnel and I will be able to spend time with my kids—and that's the thing I miss the most... I still love Katie even after what she did. I realize she was disturbed."

Commonwealth Attorney William Crockett said his office could appeal the ruling, or choose to retry Smith, even though the prosecuting witness is dead.

Crockett said his decision whether to appeal Summe's ruling, seek a new trial or let the ruling stand will require "a lot of prayer, and a lot of thought."

"It's a very difficult case," he said. "It was tried cleanly, with a jury consisting of his peers. It withstood the scrutiny of the State Supreme Court and they upheld the original conviction," Crockett explained.

He said the later developments surrounding Katie Smith's faked pregnancy, her assault on a pregnant woman and her death complicated the issues.

"You always have to wonder if the problems she had later in her life were a direct result of the abuse; or was she having difficulty dealing with reality? It's easy to arrive at assumptions when she isn't there to give her side of the story from that day onward," Crockett explained the details of the changed circumstances.

He said the abuse that Katie Smith originally accused her father of had allegedly taken place when she was seven or eight years old.

"We never want to see an innocent person in jail. He's claimed to be innocent and has from day one. That's what most people do. Some change that, but he never did," Crockett stated.

Crockett, however, reserved the right to fully review the case.

Chapter 26

Media Circus

It was 12:15 A.M. and someone was knocking on Ron Hatton's door.

He was surprised when he opened it to find a network news reporter from New York

"The reporter had just flown in, it was amazing. I wondered how big the story was going to get."

Ron, Sarah, Scott, their family and friends would find out soon enough.

The police told Sarah and Scott that what happened to Sarah would be a big local story.

"That made sense," Sarah said. "But we certainly weren't thinking it would become a national or international story."

However, one person, attorney Bob Carran, had a notion of the enormity of the story's appeal. News crews and reporters were already camped out in front of Scott and Sarah's house as well as in front of Scott's and Sarah's mothers' homes.

"You may need my help because they are all over the place," Carran phoned Sarah.

Carran wisely suggested that Sarah and Scott appoint a family spokesperson to handle interviews. They decided on Scott's brother, Ron, who appeared at ease talking on camera to reporters.

Meanwhile, the phones were ringing and more reporters were converging and hovering, each one trying to get an exclusive in-depth interview with Sarah.

In addition to the local newspapers, the *Kentucky Enquirer*, an edition of the *Cincinnati Enquirer*, the *Kentucky Post,* and the local network affiliates in Cincinnati were all attempting to interview Sarah. There were the major network and cable news shows—ABC, NBC, CBS, CNN, FOX, MSNBC, CNBC and others. It seemed like every major news organization in the country was staking out Sarah, Scott and anyone associated with them.

In addition, many talk shows such as *Oprah* and *Montel*, entertainment and magazine shows like *Inside Edition*, and even print like *National Enquirer*, were already clamoring for the story, and vied for interviews.

A tabloid contacted one of Sarah's high school friends and offered $5,000 for a picture of Sarah. The friend turned the offer down.

Newspapers from Germany, England and South America were contacting Sarah. She found the media attention both amazing and disturbing. Amid all her other concerns and the police's continuing questioning, Sarah could not escape thinking about the attack. She was concerned about the effect her constant worry would have on her unborn child and knew she had to try to calm down.

Trying to concentrate on her family well-being, Sarah began staying with Scott's grandparents in Burlington, the county seat of Boone County, a fast-growing community west of Sarah's. Escape only lasted a short time. Once the reporters found out where Sarah was staying, satellite trucks filled the street.

Scott's grandmother recalled, "One of the papers was trying to take a picture of us through the window with one of those long lenses. I called the police, and they said they were monitoring the situation, but as long as they didn't get on our property they couldn't just throw them off the street."

Reporters parked their cars near the county courthouse in Burlington and followed members of Sarah's family, hoping to catch a glimpse of Sarah. One night there was a knock at the door and outside stood a man holding a pizza.

"Except we didn't order a pizza," Scott's grandfather said. "It was a reporter, trying to get in by acting like a pizza delivery man."

For Sarah and Scott, it was almost surreal later watching the incident dissected on television and in the newspapers.

Most of the initial reporting backed Sarah's version of the attack and alleged that Smith was perpetrating a pregnancy ruse in order to steal an unborn child and make it her own.

WCPO television in Cincinnati interviewed a neighbor who lived near Katie Smith in an apartment complex in Park Hills, a small Kenton County suburb that is located between Covington and Fort Mitchell.

"When she left here, she was pregnant enough that she was showing," a former neighbor, told WCPO. "When we moved in, there was a baby seat in the hallway and a couple of books about parenting and baby care."

A woman who lives in the same Fort Mitchell apartment building as Katie told WCPO that she believed her young neighbor was pregnant.

"On the day of the attack, I came home and saw six cop cars and four ambulances on the street. I assumed the woman on the first floor was having her baby," said neighbor Amanda Arlinghaus.

The reporter also interviewed Chief Hensley and Sergeant Loos of the Fort Mitchell police.

"Katie Smith had a complete nursery, all of the furniture, baby clothes, diapers, formula—everything a parent expecting a newborn should have," Loos said. "We're fortunate in this case. There's plenty for us to follow up on and we're going to get a clear picture before it's finished."

Loos said it appeared that Sarah was giving a truthful account of the attack based on the injuries she sustained in the fight.

"I would characterize the wounds Sarah exhibited to be similar to defensive wounds I've seen in the past," he said.

Loos said as part of his investigation he spoke to several members of Katie's family. They thought she was pregnant but the young woman apparently told conflicting stories about when the child was due to be born.

Katie appeared to be timing the alleged birth to her

planned attack on Brady.

"I talked to about thirteen family members who called me," Loos told the television station. "She kept moving the delivery date forward."

"As we understand it," Hensley said during the interview, "Ms. Brady was in fact pregnant and the other young lady was not."

In that same report the commentator talked to Scott's mother, who said she and other family members are convinced Katie was going to kill Sarah and steal her baby.

"She turned out to be a psycho," Scott's mother said.

In an interview with another Cincinnati television station, WKRC, Loos described how most of the necessary equipment to deliver a baby was found in Katie's apartment.

"These are typical items that we would expect to see in an (obstetrics) kit that EMS crews typically have," Loos said while displaying the items during the interview. "This is an umbilical clip that's attached to the umbilical cord after delivery, hemostats, a pair of surgical gloves and of course, absorbent pads."

It was reported that police also found what was described as a "pregnancy pillow" that Smith apparently wore to convince her family that she was about to have a baby.

Loos, who seemed to be all over the airwaves in the days following the attack, said in another interview that Sarah's story about being attacked held up.

"We did not find anything that would give us cause to be concerned about Sarah Brady's version of the facts," he said.

One question remained as to why Sarah, a bright and grounded person, trusted Katie Smith to perform the delivery of her baby?

Prosecutor Bill Crockett, in a report, called the situation "a horrific case, a very sad ending to her life."

With so much attention on Sarah, Bob Carran and his partner Phil Taliaferro, decided on a media strategy the day after the attack, a Friday. Speculation was already swirling about the incident, including a false and disturbing rumor that Scott had an affair with Katie Smith and that she and Sarah were fighting over him. Needless to say this rumor really upset Sarah.

Sarah needed to tell her side of the story. The lawyers suggested that she talk to one or two of the local television stations and one of the morning network talk shows. *Good Morning America,* which had requested an interview, was the chosen talk show.

Sarah agreed to do the *Good Morning America* interview from the Hatton's living room. Respected host Kate Snow would interview Sarah very early on Monday morning.

Crews arrived at the Hatton home about four in the morning to start setting up. Producers told Sarah she would do the interview with Snow and it would be played just a few minutes later on the air. Carran and Taliaferro were telling Sarah to stay calm. "Don't let them get anything from you that you don't want to talk about," Sarah recalls being told by the lawyers.

Good Morning America actually wanted to do the interview live, but Sarah was concerned about breaking down and crying. "I didn't want to lose it on national television."

So the producers compromised on the taped interview, with Sawyer in New York asking questions and Sarah answering from the living room in Scott's grandmother's house.

"I have the most famous wall in America," Scott's grandmother joked later about the living room wall that was used for Sarah's backdrop.

During the interview, Sarah, nervous but outwardly composed, dutifully answered Sawyer's questions on what happened in the apartment. Inside, however, Sarah's stomach churned and her heart beat so rapidly she felt it would be audible.

"She did appear to look pregnant. The only thing I thought," Sarah said during the interview, "was that she was going to kill me and my child. I was able to get the knife away from her after several minutes of struggling. Unfortunately, she was wounded and didn't make it."

At one point Sarah talked lovingly of the daughter she was carrying. She promised that even the near fatal attack wouldn't interfere with the baby's normal birth.

"The child is going to bring something wonderful to me. She was definitely meant to be in this world."

Sarah said she became suspicious of Smith after noticing her name on the inhaler and the formula coupons.

"At that point I knew something was wrong," she said.

Sarah also reconfirmed that the fight started after Smith gave her a hug.

"That's when she pulled out the knife," Sarah told the national television audience.

Good Morning America also interviewed Chief

Hensley for the story. He described their theory that Sarah fought back courageously after Smith brandished the knife.

Hensley outlined the way in which Sarah could have gotten control of the situation, "She was able to knock the knife out of her hand and it ultimately hit the floor for a short time."

"Smith retrieved the knife and again tried to stab Brady, who managed to turn the knife of her attacker," the officer went on.

In the same interview, ABC's reporter talked to one of Smith's neighbors who agreed with Sarah that Katie Smith appeared to be pregnant.

"She had a pair of khakis and a blue jean maternity shirt. She looked visibly pregnant," the neighbor told the reporter.

Police confirmed during the program that an autopsy revealed Smith had never been pregnant. Her pregnancy, police said, was a "farce."

Sergeant Loos from the Fort Mitchell police was also interviewed, calling what happened between Sarah and Smith "an extremely bizarre case."

"Katie Smith had a complete nursery with all the furniture," Loos said during the interview. "She had baby clothes, diapers, and formula—everything that a parent expecting a newborn should have."

Sarah stated in the interview that while she feared for her life during the attack, she also felt the fear helped her fight off Smith's attack. Sarah also said she felt "blessed."

Loos also told the *Associated Press* that Katie "was mentally disturbed" and "clearly obsessed with motherhood."

And he told the *Kentucky Enquirer* that Katie was con-vincing in pulling off her alleged pregnancy.

"It's amazing how good she was at deception, probably because she believed it all at some level," he said.

In the weeks and even months that passed after the attack, Sarah, Scott and their families got a rare glimpse of how once the media finds the public intrigued by a story, they won't let go. And they were shocked at the continuing attention.

"I know reporters have a job to do," said family spokes-man. "But dealing with them really enforces what a lot of people think about the media -that they'll do anything to get the story and don't really care about the people involved.

"You hear them on television saying their hearts go out to the victim or whatever," the spokesman said. "Well, I talked to a lot of them on the phone, and most of all they want their story and they'll do anything and say anything to get it."

In today's world, media has to include internet web logs or blogs, where just about anyone with a computer can post their comments about any subject or news event. They too sought out Sarah and her family and friends relentlessly.

Sarah's story and her battle with Katie Smith obviously intrigued the public. Most of the comments favored Sarah and were extremely critical of Katie.

Someone who identified himself as "safety guy" thanked "mom for a job well done! I think her child is in very good hands."

In another posting, "English Leigh" commented on the disturbing trend of attacks on pregnant women.

"This is getting far too commonplace. Ladies out there who are pregnant, be very careful!"

One blogger from Michigan contributed his own strong feelings about the case saying, "Good for her. I thank GOD she and the baby are both alright. You know if she was here in Michigan she would have probably gone to jail. I am just so glad that she and baby are fine. Good, for her, that's a mother of a woman!"

Others felt equally empassioned expressing the following:

"People are so crazy . . . you always need to be careful."

"I'm glad she survived, and if killing the woman was necessary to protect herself and her baby then so be it."

"It's far better for the would-be murderess to die than the intended victim. I still feel sorry for the pregnant woman, though, even though she survived. That must have been a horrific experience."

"I find it amazing that a nine-month pregnant woman was able to kill a woman. I guess it's a mother's instincts. Good job, mom."

Time inched by but public interest in Sarah, her unborn child and the bizarre attack didn't diminish.

"It just went on and on, it's still going on, we get calls every week, sometimes every day, from people who want to do interviews," Sarah said in August of 2005, many months after the attack.

Chapter 27

Roots of Disturbance

Was Katie Smith desperate for attention? Or was she desperate to become a mother? Regardless of her underlying motives, her actions proved her to be a severely disturbed individual. Did the system fail Katie? Had she been able to reach out would she have been met with profession-alism and compassion?

Growing up with two alcoholic parents in an unstable and unhealthy environment must have had a major impact on the psychotic adult into which Katie developed. Could Katie Smith have been labeled as the "scapegoat" in her maladaptive family situation?

According to co-dependency therapist Robert Burney, a child who acts as a scapegoat "provides distraction from the real issues in the family. The scapegoat usually has trouble in school because they get attention the only way they know how -which is negatively. They often become pregnant or addicted as a teenager. They have a lot of hatred and can be very self destructive."

However, Katie Smith took the scapegoat persona to a higher, more bizarre level. Many questions and theories come to mind, among them: Why did she fake a pregnancy instead of becoming pregnant?

It's possible that she did try to get pregnant and was unable to do so. Or, since she alleged she was sexually abused by her father, maybe this fantasy caused her to fear involving herself with a man. Perhaps she feared the act of sex, and conjectured that she would have to steal the child she so desperately wanted in order to have one for herself. Maybe the concept of acquiring a child on her own, without the necessity of a man, was strangely appealing to Katie's distorted mind.

Katie may have been so accustomed to her role as a mother figure to her siblings or her contorted perception of herself led her to believe that she could only be a parent and not a daughter or sister. It's possible from many reports of her past history that Smith was never truly able to have a real childhood.

As a child, Katie may have witnessed violence either physical or emotional toward her mother by her father. In turn, she may have viewed pregnant women as an outlet to release anger. Or, she might have hated her mother, because she resented having to care for her siblings. It's also possible that Katie saw her mother pregnant and felt hostility towards her, because Katie felt further displaced each time her mother had another baby.

If Katie Smith had her own baby, she would have complete control over the love between her and 'her' child. However, both her sisters and Sarah's child were not her own children. Did Katie feel self-loathing and not want a child that came from her own womb?

It's surprising that Katie's cries for attention or cries for help were not taken more seriously by both medical professionals and the high school staff. Katie may have received the help she needed had she lived in an area in which more children would be referred for psychological services.

Social worker Gary Kummer states, "A social worker would normally assign a psychologist and psychiatrist for someone in Katie's situation, and she would be placed in foster care. It's possible that the state system was overworked. Somewhere along the line Katie must've fallen through the gaps, and in turn, ignored by medical and mental health professionals."

Psychiatrist Dr. Richard Rice also expands on this point stating that if Katie did in fact have a history of violent behavior, she would have been a likely candidate for psychological treatment. However, it appears that nobody took her seriously since her behavior never reached the level where she would be sent to the hospital and mandated treatment. However, that she was mentally unstable was certain. While lots of children feign illness for attention, Katie needed attention to the point of being psychotic, actually demanding exploratory surgery. Maybe Katie viewed the surgery on her abdomen as a way to almost feel like she was pregnant and receiving a Cesarean.

Is there some correlation between Katie's own scar on her stomach and her plan of cutting open another woman's stomach? Did her mother receive a Cesarean at one point in time? If she did, Katie may have desired to perform a 'Cesarean' on someone else to free herself of pent up anger and aggressive feelings toward her mother.

According to author Sieglinde Songer, mental illness and other psychological problems are common among children in dysfunctional families. So, it's no surprise that Katie Smith had severe psychological problems. Children who live in turbulent home environments are more likely to become murderers or perpetrators of violent crimes. *A Review of the Literature*, Rudo and Powell. As far as we know, Katie did not have any history of violence. But the question why Katie would resort to extreme brutality only to obtain a child to call her own has posed many theories. Katie most likely had access to medications and needles at the hospital where she worked; why didn't she drug Sarah instead of attempting to murder her? Speculations on Katie's motivation for committing this crime cause further questions. No doubt her motivation had its roots in something more than alcoholic parents. Did some event set her off? Who modeled violence for her?

Psychiatrist Dr. Richard Rice states, "Though it remains unknown whether Katie's father truly abused her, the fact that Katie *believed* her father abused her could have contributed to her psychotic behavior. She may not have been able to distinguish between fantasy and reality." Katie may have assembled the disconcerting ideas by herself, but in her mind there *was* sexual abuse.

According to Vernon Geberth, a retired lieutenant-commander of the New York City Police Department, Katie Smith does not fit the standard profile of a fetus attacker. Geberth states that the fundamental objective in the majority of fetus attacks is to "sustain a relationship with a male partner by providing them with a child."

This was not the case with Katie Smith. It seems as though Katie wanted Sarah Brady's child only for herself. To all appearances she simply seemed to have an intense desire to be a mother. Smith probably did not have any intentions of presenting a significant other with the baby. Geberth offers a pertinent insight; he explains that the offenders often feel they are in essence becoming the infant's mother when physically obtaining a baby through the vicious method of kidnapping by Cesarean. This explains why Smith did not choose to simply steal a baby from the hospital where she was employed. Nevertheless, Katie's work at Saint Elizabeth Hospital could have been an influential factor in preparing her with the necessary experience to deliver a baby.

Geberth explains that the perpetrators in these crimes are usually not insane under the law since they are well aware of their actions which are usually very thought out and planned beforehand.

Geberth states, "There have been nine attacks on pregnant women since 1987. There have been at least three assaults on an expectant mother for her child since 2003."

It seems strange that all of these incidents took place within a fifteen-year time span. These perverse crimes seemed to have increased since 1987. Since the crimes have been so publicized in the media, psychotic women may have seen this type of crime as a way to get attention, a baby and possibly release hostile or jealous feelings onto a pregnant woman.

The Montgomery attack in Kansas occurred only two months prior to Katie Smith's attempted murder and kid-napping. The Peggy Jo Connor attack happened shortly after Smith's attack was exposed to the public. These murders not only follow similar patterns, but also seem to have a domino type effect. Is this simply coincidence? Or are these criminals "copycat" murderers?

One website wikipedia states, "The 'copycat effect' refers to the tendency of sensational publicity about a violent murder or suicide to cause more of the same."

According to Aimee Lewis in her report entitled, *The Ancient Art of Violence*, violence in film is often thought to elicit copycat crimes. A taxicab driver in Belgian admitted to the fact that he was inspired by the film *Scream* after committing a vicious copycat murder of a teenager. He went to the extent of wearing the Scream outfit while killing the young woman.

Loren Coleman, author of *The Copycat Effect*, explains that violence displayed in the media is "triggering vulnerable and angry people to take their own lives and that of others." Copycat murders, Coleman asserts, are often spawned by media sensationalism of murders such as that of Jack the Ripper in the late 1880s and the "going postal" massacres of mail service employees one hundred years later.

Should violence displayed in the media be regulated? Or is it simply a part of reality that the media shouldn't have to conceal? Has graphic cruelty become so readily accepted in present day society? It seems that a nonchalant response is not an uncommon reaction to bloodshed, and in turn, the elevated shock value appears to have become a priority in both film and in the news.

On the other hand, Aimee Lewis believes, "Films must be allowed to comment on the brutal elements of society and if parents don't want their children to see these violent films, then they should be able to rely on the ratings system."

Would society improve if we were ignorant of such criminal acts? Or is it beneficial to publicize violence, so as to keep the general public aware of these incidents? If a restriction were to be placed on the media's open exposure of cruelty, would the crime rate drop? Or would this type of chain reaction never have existed?

In any case, it appears to be very likely that the fetus attacks were of a copycat nature. It's quite or very possible that Katie Smith and the other fetus snatchers never would have performed these atrocious offenses had others not committed similar crimes which they heard about and which played into their desires.

Dr. Richard Rice speculates, "It is possible that Katie Smith may have attempted to commit a copycat crime. She might have seen this as a way of solving her needs for a child."

This seems probable, because Katie had been contemplating pregnancy since her high school years. Most likely, Katie was aware of the fact that she would not be allowed to adopt a child given her past history of pseudo illnesses and pregnancies and her lack of financial resources. Stealing a baby from a hospital may have felt too sterile or she may not have felt she could pull this off and, even if she could, this would not have provided her with the corporeal nature of the act that she longed for. In all likelihood, Katie had heard or read of a similar kidnapping and used this as an outline to begin to plan every detail of her own diabolical scheme step by step.

Chapter 28

The Most Anticipated Birth

Sarah was unable to sleep.

As the days passed, Sarah was still suffering stress from the attack and from Katie Smith's death. She couldn't bring herself to face the repeated demands of the media, which continued to camp out in front of her house; she felt like a prisoner and she wouldn't venture outside, even canceling doctor's appointments because of the trauma she had suffered.

Though she was worried about her family, concerned about whether she would ever feel her old optimistic self and exhausted, Sarah told herself that it was the baby she had to put first. On February 14, 2005 she forced herself to make another doctor's appointment. Other than telling her the baby's birth was delayed—Sarah's original due date was February 3, 2005—the doctor, Dr. Steven Willett, said Sarah and her child appeared to be doing fine. For Sarah, his findings were not only a relief, but helped her focus on the one bright spot in her life, the baby's impending birth. Sarah longed for that.

Dr. Willett noted in his office record:

"Patient requests induction at hospital, St. Elizabeth Medical Center, because of persistent media coverage. Per her request, I will schedule induction at St. Elizabeth Hospital contacted and made aware of her situation. They will provide increased security and privacy measures for her."

However, Sarah didn't have to wait long. Her contractions started that night. But the birth wasn't going to happen momentarily, "The contractions were much too far apart and weren't strong enough as yet."

The waiting game was on for what had to be the most anticipated birth in America at the time. Twenty four hours passed. By the next night, Tuesday, the contractions were coming every six minutes. Sarah and Scott headed to St. Elizabeth, where she was admitted at about 10:30 P.M.

As she was prepared, Sarah tried to take deep breaths and relax, but she couldn't.

The nurse gave her some medication, but it didn't do much good.

"That should have knocked you out," the nurse told Sarah.

But by then it wasn't stress that was keeping Sarah awake, it was heavy labor pains that were intensifying.

At that point, Sarah was given an epidural, a common method used by doctors in childbirth. The spine is injected with a regional anesthetic to numb the abdomen, genital area and pelvis.

Suddenly, a complication arose. Somehow between

the ultrasound taken a week previously and labor, the baby had flipped while inside Sarah's womb. "Sunny side up" as Sarah later put it.

The ideal birthing position is known as anterior, when the back of the baby's head is toward the front of the mother's abdomen. In this posture the baby's head is looking down when the infant passes through the birth canal.

But Sarah's baby was now posterior. The back of the infant's head was pointing toward the mother's spine.

Worried about the baby's condition, Sarah asked herself when the change had occurred. It had to be during her savage fight with Katie Smith, Sarah thought. Not only had the attack turned her own world upside down, it also affected her unborn child.

Sarah was pushing to get the baby out, but nothing was happening. The decision was made to take the baby through a Cesarean or C-section. The doctor had Sarah prepared for surgery and the anesthesia administered.

Throughout the ordeal, Scott was with Sarah. Then at 1:16 P.M. a happy ending: Mckaila Grace came into the world weighing seven pounds, four ounces. In a curiously ironic twist, Sarah had given birth at the same institution Katie Smith once worked, St. Elizabeth Medical Center. Dr. Willett, Sarah's OB/GYN, noted in the medical records:

"This patient had been through a traumatic experience late in her third trimester and suffered significant trauma. She is just a few days postdate and I elected to induce her because of the recent trauma and the fact that she was term uterine pregnancy. She had an uncomplicated prenatal course until the traumatic incident in the third trimester."

Sarah originally wanted to name the baby Emma, but Scott didn't really care for the name. When he saw *Mckaila* written on a wall in the maternity ward where the names of babies are posted, he thought it beautiful and fitting, and Sarah agreed.

Sarah always liked the name Grace. She and Scott chose that for the baby's middle name after discovering that Scott's great grandmother's middle name was also Grace. The baby's name would be Mckaila Grace. A crowd of family and friends were at the hospital, anxiously awaiting the arrival of the baby who had provoked so much interest around the world.

"Scott's mom was there; my mom was there; his grandfather and his grandma were there; both of his brothers were there, his sister-in-law, his brother's girlfriend. Twenty five people were there at the hospital plus reporters and media, waiting for me to have this baby."

Throughout Sarah's stay and to primarily keep reporters and unwanted visitors away, the hospital posted a security guard outside of Sarah's hospital door around the clock. Family members joked that even they couldn't get in, and a few did have to show identification before visiting the mother and her newborn daughter.

The funny thing was that the guards didn't recognize Scott from one visit to the next. "Every time

Scott came in and out," Sarah said, "he had to pull out his ID."

To throw reporters off Sarah's trail she had been admitted to the hospital under a false name. The phone was also turned off in Sarah's hospital room, a move made to ensure no media could get through to Sarah and disturb her rest. None of these deceptive devices worked.

The media rooted out Sarah's location and converged at the hospital.

Reporters were feverishly jockeying to get interviews with the new mom and a picture or video of baby Mckaila, but Scott and Sarah wanted to keep their happy event private and personal. They had had enough media attention to last forever and felt the trauma and anxiety should end. They wanted to give their new baby peace and security.

But the calls kept coming from *Inside Edition, Maurey Povich*, the *Early Show, Prime Time Live, Fox News*, CNN, NBC, the *National Enquirer*, and the British press. It seemed like every major media outlet, show or personality probably tried to get the story. When they saw the competition, the stakes went up.

One tabloid offered $5,000.00 for a picture of the baby. Others contacted Sarah's high school friends, offering money for pictures of Sarah and information about her.

Sarah and Scott begged for privacy. The hospital cooperated, placing Sarah away from the news pack. On the day Mckaila and Sarah were to go home, they put her and the baby in a wheel chair and took them out that Friday through an area under construction for a hospital expansion. It was all only a postponement.

"There was media everywhere around the hospital," Sarah said. "So they wheeled me through what looked like a tunnel and through an area that was being worked on. We got away, but as soon as we got home we saw TV trucks parked all over the street and the reporters started calling as soon as we entered the front door."

Sarah wanted to put the circus out of her mind: the traumatic events leading to Katie Smith's death, the media, and the police, but it seemed impossible. Still, holding their little baby in her arms with Scott at her side and her family all around her helped ease the emotional and physical pain Sarah had been feeling since the savage attack. She felt this the happiest moment she had ever experienced. She let out a sigh of relief. She saved her Grace and grace had saved her.

The future was more important than the past. Scott and Sarah were talking about when they would marry. They rented a new house in Taylor Mill, a community that abuts Covington. Scott's son had decided having a little sister was very exciting and he was anxious to show her off.

Sarah worried a lot about the effects of stress on her and her young family. Sarah knew that the ordeal with Katie Smith was a traumatic and horrible event that would be forever branded in their memories. But she told herself that's what it was, just a memory. It was over. It was time for her partner and her to bond together with their new baby and to make their home a secure and happy one for the two children. She prayed they could.

Chapter 29

Swirling Maelstrom

Hopes, plans, and aspirations swirled in their heads as Scott and Sarah celebrated the birth of their new baby and tried to adjust to all the myriad tasks of having her home and caring for the the infant. But despite their attempts to settle down into a happy, normal family life, more turmoil occurred. When Katie Smith attacked Sarah and her unborn child, Sarah became the center of a storm of controversy. The investigation dragged on and on. Sarah Brady was not charged with a crime. But rumors and accusations from the family of the dead woman kept appearing. Sarah wanted the case closed and her named cleared. But that didn't happen. Instead the storm intensified. She endured news reports that the entire fight with Katie Smith was over a man or that Sarah wanted money. Both allegations were untrue. But frustration after frustration mounted as the attorney her brother called for couldn't get the mess cleared up and over with. Who would help her? Who could? Sometimes answers appear from unlikely places.

Several years prior to the attack, Sarah had served on a jury in a medical malpractice case in Kenton County. The case involved the death of a small boy. The issue involved whether a doctor failed to properly treat and admit an infant who had what is called an apparent life threatening event from gastric reflux. Sarah argued in the jury room against the doctor. The jury was deadlocked six to six. The vote needed to be at least nine to three either way. After three hours of deliberation and the time reaching 5:00 P.M. on a Friday, Sarah Brady informed the other jurors she was switching her vote. Two others followed suit. The trial was over.

Immediately after the trial, Eric Deters, the lawyer for the deceased boy's family, met with the three jurors who voted for the family. They were stunned at what happened.

"Mr. Deters. The girl who argued most for you just switched her vote."

Feeling sympathy for the family, Eric Deters began calling jurors, meeting jurors and obtaining affidavits from jurors. His hope was for a new trial or successful appeal. Where was the justice in an outcome like this?

He reached Sarah Brady by telephone. She agreed to meet him at her home. He found her house down a small side street in the heart of Covington. She welcomed him in. The home was cluttered but cozy. It was obvious it was the humble abode of a working man. Work boots and tools were on the porch.

As Eric and Sarah exchanged small talk while he

settled himself in a comfortable chair, Eric asked Sarah about the jury deliberations. She expressed regret that she had capitulated when in her heart she really believed that the doctor was at fault. She was also willing to sign an affidavit, which she did.

It was all too late. A request for a new trial, appeals to the Kentucky Court of Appeals and the Kentucky Supreme Court failed. One shot. It was unfair. But that's how it goes. It happens all the time. But this doesn't make the event less tragic, especially for the family of the deceased child.

Eric never spoke to Sarah Brady again. Then, one evening, after a long day at work, Eric sat down in his living room to read the local evening newspaper. The story about a woman fighting for her life to save her baby from being stolen from her womb caught his attention. He saw the name Sarah Brady. He saw the photograph. The name. The picture. It seemed familiar. Where had he heard the name and seen this woman?

Finally, it clicked. Sarah Brady was the juror who had voted against his client. He knew this woman who had killed to protect her baby. Having long ago forgiven her, because she tried to undo her mistake at the doctor's trial, he picked up the phone and called her. He got her answering machine and voice mail.

"Sarah, this is Eric Deters. You may remember I was the attorney on the medical malpractice case you sat on. I just wanted you to know I appreciated how you tried to right the wrong to my clients in that case and if I can help you out in any way, please call me. Thanks."

As the days passed and Sarah's story was in the paper every day, Eric read Sarah had an attorney. He believed she was in good hands. It sounded as if she didn't do anything wrong. He never expected to hear from her. Then one day, out of the blue, he received a voice mail:

"Eric, this is Sarah Brady. You left me a message; I'd like to talk to you. Please call me."

Eric telephoned Sarah and they scheduled a meeting at her house. When they met, Sarah related what had happened and told Eric of the continuing upheaval swirling about her and the fact that she had two main concerns. She wanted the investigation over and the case closed. Her name should be cleared. She didn't understand the delay. She also was still being bombarded with news and press requests. Major news and talk shows in the United States still wanted the story. Sarah didn't know what to do.

First Eric asked her why she didn't have an attorney. Sarah said that she did, but she was frustrated with them. "They keep telling me to be patient. I'm tired of being patient. I've done nothing wrong. I want this over with so my family and I can get on with our lives and recover from this horrible trauma."

Eric informed her he knew the police, the prosecutor and her attorneys. He would make a few calls for her and find out what was happening. He called the police, the prosecutor and her attorney. After speaking to them, he counseled Sarah that time would be needed to resolve this convoluted and difficult case. Sarah insisted she needed representation with the press, and had none. Eric agreed to help her. Soon he was representing Sarah on all fronts.

Chapter 30

Troubling Allegations

Meanwhile the police continued to ply Sarah with questions. Both large and small issues kept cropping up. They even questioned her about her green Jeep Cherokee. Apparently, someone reported to the police they had seen one for months near the address in Fort Mitchell where Katie Smith lived. Sarah asked them: "What's your point?" She told them, "Give me dates and times and I'll tell you where I was."

A short while later the police responded: "Well, we checked it out. There are a lot of green jeeps." That was an obvious answer to an easy question.

The police then returned to the "baby broker" allegation of Katie Smith's family. The new allegation was Sarah gave Katie $500.00 here, $200.00 there until the total sum of $5,000.00 was paid. The claims inflamed Sarah.

Apparently, Katie had claimed, "Allegedly, our agreement was that I was going to go to her house, deliver the baby there, she was going to take it and resell the baby."

Sarah stared at the officer and said:

"I thought we covered all this; are you serious?"

The police assured her they dismissed the overall allegation, because no one ever sold a baby for less than $10,000! Also, single moms are usually involved, not mothers in relationships.

However, the other things being said were even more troubling. The Katie Smith family allegation was Sarah showed up on that fateful day, didn't want to give the baby up, and didn't want to give the money back, so she killed Katie. This astonished Sarah. The police told her they were covering all the bases, because someone died. Sarah gave an emotional response:

"She's not the victim. I don't care which way you look at it. Yes, she is dead, but I'm the victim. I'm the one that has to live with this for the rest of my life. I didn't do this to her. She did this to me."

She began to cry. Not able to stop herself she blurted out between sobs, "Here I almost lost my life and my baby's (life), and they are trying to say I wanted to sell my baby," she said.

At this point, Sarah began to fear some members of Katie Smith's family. Then other bizarre behavior gave Sarah more reason to be concerned. Scott's mother worked at a convenience store in Covington across from Holmes High School, which Scott and Sarah had attended years before. Several women came to the store and asked weird questions about Sarah, Scott and the baby. And even more worrisome, they knew where Sarah and her young family were living. One morning, not long after Scott's mother told her about the incidents, Sarah walked out the front door of her house intending to take a little walk with the baby. Suddenly, hearing snatches of loud conversation, she looked around. People were milling about outside of her house. They were pointing to Sarah and the baby. Covering her little one's head with the blanket she had swirled about her, Sarah began to shake uncontrollably. She rushed back inside her house.

Later Sarah was recognized when she went to see Scott's mother at the convenience store. "I had a man come in and stand in the aisle right behind me," Sarah said. "It was frightening and I stopped going out alone at that point, because I was so worried about the safety of my little baby."

Chapter 31

Truth and Consequences

Sarah's prior lawyers were excellent criminal defense attorneys. They had advised Sarah *not* to take a lie detector test. This is usually good advice for any "suspect." However, her new attorney, Eric Deters, took a different approach. He asked Sarah this question:

"Are you guilty of anything improper?"

"Absolutely not," responded Sarah.

"Well, then, I want you to take the test," Eric replied.

Eric's reasons were twofold. First, more than anything, Sarah wanted the investigation over and she wanted to be removed as a suspect to any crime. With her permission, Eric called the police and Bill Crockett, the prosecutor. Crockett informed him he was not going to take any further steps in the investigation unless the police presented it to him. The police stated that if Sarah took the test and passed, unless something else "fell in their lap," they would have no reason to keep the case open.

The second reason Eric wanted Sarah to take the test was to remove any doubt in public opinion and to refute the allegations he felt were false of some of Katie Smith's family. Under Kentucky law, passing or failing a polygraph test is not admissible in a criminal or civil trial. However, public suspicions rise when someone refuses to take the test. Does public sympathy rise when someone passes the test? Sarah decided that Eric had a very good point and she was anxious to do as he asked.

Eric Deters called Chief Hensley to communicate Sarah's decision to take the test. It was scheduled with the Ohio State Police on August 15, 2005.

She told herself although taking such a test was scary there was no reason for her to worry about the results. Although Sarah felt anxious, she knew she had told the police everything. In her mind she flashed back to the awful incident. Katie Smith falsely identified herself and lured Sarah into a trap of deception and lies. Sarah simply had defended herself and refused to submit to the usual outcome where the victim normally doesn't make it out alive. In past cases of fetus theft, there had not been a reported attack where the victim survived and the attacker died. Sarah wanted everyone to know without a doubt that she was telling the complete truth.

On August 15, 2005, Eric Deters met Sarah at the test site in Dayton, Ohio. It surprised Sarah when she found out the test would take considerable time. Her nerves were shot. She worried about the accuracy of the test. She kept murmuring to herself: "What if this says I am lying, because I wasn't?" Only Sarah was allowed in the room, so Eric Deters left after reassuring Sarah that all would turn out alright. The examiner, Detective Slusher, was a clean-cut man in his early thirties. He showed no emotion, quickly diving into a line of questions to help steer through the course of action needed to provide an accurate reading. She tried to hide the fear and anguish that filled inside her. Her pulse was beating quickly. To Sarah, it felt as if her heart would beat right out of her chest. Her palms were cold and wet with sweat.

Sarah could feel trickles of sweat rolling down her back as the examiner dug deep into her intimate life. She was quite astounded at the line of questioning. They wanted to know about her personal background, lies that she had told in the past, people she had wronged and her relationship with her loved ones. What had this line of questioning to do with the reason she was there? She did everything in her power to hold back her anguished emotions. Nevertheless, she wanted answers as to the legitimacy of these types of questions. Several unanswered questions lingered in her mind. Finally she burst out asking the examiner, "Why does it matter if I ever lied before, or how my relationship with Scott is progressing?"

The examiner answered that they used these preliminary questions and their answers to gather information. They needed to determine the state of Sarah's emotions. They had to decide whether or not she was highly emotional or not, in order to correctly read and interpret the results of the test. "You will understand this better once I actually conduct the test."

After three and a half grueling hours the examiner

was called out of the office having received a note that his wife had to go to the hospital. When he came back he apologized to Sarah but said he had to excuse himself and not give her the rest of the test. They would have to finish on Wednesday. Sarah was upset, but she understood better than most how a family emergency could interfere and that he needed to be with his wife. Walking out of the Ohio State Police patrol office, Sarah called a friend to come and pick her up.

The young woman agreed to drive Sarah home. Considering Sarah's frayed nerves, the friend believed it best she drive.

Sarah stood outside the building waiting patiently for her friend when she turned to see a man who looked familiar standing in front of her. It was Detective Scott Nottingham from the Fort Mitchell Police. He appeared a little embarrassed, his face immediately turned red. He started stammering questions at Sarah, "Do you need a ride? How did you feel about the test?" It was obviously a plot to distract attention from why he was there in the first place. Nevertheless, Sarah couldn't help thinking he had obviously been there either listening or waiting for the examiner to report back to him about the findings of the test results. Seeing Detective Nottingham's face made Sarah sick to her stomach. The churning would not go away for several days.

Sarah felt betrayed. Especially the fact that her lawyer, Eric Deters, was not allowed to be present during the questioning made her feel like she was being railroaded. What more did the police want? She had given them everything they asked for. She opened up her personal private affairs. Her whole life was there for them to pick apart.

Agonizing, Sarah grew angry. A rage had been building over the last six months. She despised how the police and the prosecutor were acting, how they were treating her. She resented being treated like a criminal. After she left, Sarah began to feel ill.

She had agreed to meet with the examiner two more times, but both meetings were canceled due to his personal family illness. Sarah became more distraught; when was it all going to end and how?

On August 19, 2005, Friday of that same week, she was scheduled to meet with the examiner early that afternoon. They were in the last stages of the process. The examiner performed some validity test to ensure he knew how to accurately read the results. As Sarah watched him she saw that the man's demeanor never changed. He had an icy aura that followed with him as he spoke. His lack of emotion made Sarah more agitated. She could not glean from him an understanding of how he felt about her case. And she wanted to be believed.

The truth of it all was the examiner wasn't supposed to have made an assumption about what occurred on that day. If he made conclusions he could not honestly read the results without some sort of bias. Of course, Sarah was unaware of all that. But even if she had known, it would have been little comfort. What she needed was affirmation, belief that others understood she had acted from necessity. All she had done was wage a just battle to save herself and her child. When these were not forthcoming she felt desolate; nevertheless, she did her best to act stoic and be wholly truthful. And when the test finally ended, Sarah felt her burden lighten at least momentarily.

Major R.W. Booker, a Commander of the Office of Investigative Services for the Ohio State Police, issued an extensive report:

On August 15, 2005, Sarah A. Brady, age twenty-six of Taylor Mill, Kentucky appeared at our District Eight Investigations Office in West Chester to be examined on the polygraph, a detection of deception technique.

Previous arrangements for this examination were made at the request of Detective Scott Nottingham with the Fort Mitchell, Kentucky Police Department.

The purpose of this examination was to determine if Sarah A. Brady had told the complete truth when she alleged that she was attacked and defended herself from a person that she knew as "Sarah Brody," later found to be Katie Smith.

Complete case facts are contained in Fort Mitchell, Kentucky Police Department report #1305000830, which is on file with their department.

Prior to the polygraph examination but during the pre-test interview, this polygraph examination had to be terminated due to personal reasons.

This examination was conducted with the understanding the results would be confidential as guided by the rules under the Ohio Public Records law.

Sarah A. Brady was examined on the polygraph using standard polygraph technique and procedure which consisted of four separate tests. The following are the pertinent questions asked Sarah A. Brady during her polygraph examination, followed by her answers to them.

> *Q. Did Katie Smith really attack you first with that knife?*
> *A. Yes.*
> *Q. Did you attack Katie Smith first with that knife?*
> *A. No.*
> *Q. Did Katie Smith really introduce herself to you as Sarah Brody?*
> *A. Yes.*
> *Q. Did Katie Smith physically try to keep you from leaving her apartment?*
> *A. Yes.*

After a careful interpretation of Sarah A. Brady's polygraph tracings, it is my opinion that no deception was indicated on her answers to the pertinent questions.

This examination was conducted with the understanding the results would be confidential as guided by the rules under the Ohio Public Records Law.

Another police officer also reviewed the results. He concluded that, overall, Ms. Brady was being truthful.

Chapter 32

Stress Filled Days and Nights

As more months passed after the attack, Sarah continued to struggle with ongoing dark thoughts of the horrors that occurred on that cold February day in Katie Smith's apartment.

Much of the time it wasn't depression but emotional turmoil which continued to haunt her.

"For a long time I cried every day. All I did was cry, cry and cry. I'll be honest, I had dreams, I had nightmares, but the more I talked about my feelings of guilt about Katie Smith's death, the better I felt. When I was silent I just bottled it up and it ate away at me. And I couldn't live like that."

Sarah was reclusive while the media hordes pursued her. Eventually, the media pursuit toned down. Sarah eventually ventured out of Scott's grandparents house in Burlington, where she was staying a lot of the time, to Scott's son's basketball games, to the store, to fix up the house she and Scott were renting in Taylor Mill, another Kenton County suburb.

But she didn't go out a lot. "We played a lot of Scrabble and Boggle at Scott's mom's house."

Yet whenever Sarah did go out, visions of the attack continued to reverberate in her mind triggered by innocuous things—a sight, a smell, a taste.

When she and Scott would arrive at their home, Sarah begged Scott to check it out before she went inside.

"I have to go in first," Scott said. "I have to walk through the entire house, including the basement, and everywhere to make sure nothing has changed, nothing has moved, nobody is in there."

Even in late August, a full six months after the attack, Sarah was still experiencing what she called "bad days."

"Some are worse than others. Some days I'm fine, other days I'm very fearful of what might happen. Like today, I had to feed the dog and let her out. To do that, all I had to do was go to our house, and then come back to Burlington. "But I had to call my mom to meet me. It was one of those terrible days."

It was certainly understandable for Sarah to have some lingering paranoia. She had been through the traumatic ordeal of being pregnant and attacked by a deranged person with a knife and then having to save herself and her unborn baby by fighting to the death with that person. Not only that, but the story continued to be highlighted in newspapers, on the news and on television talk and tabloid shows across the nation and overseas.

Her fears multiplied.

People stared. They recognized her from the news, stared at the baby and then begin whispering and pointing. It happened at a bowling alley; it happened at the grocery store.

Sarah's and Scott's families provided a strong support network for them during the days, weeks and months that followed. Scott's grandparents opened their home to Sarah and Mckalia Grace as several other family members and even friends offered encouragement and assistance.

"There were days when it seemed like twenty-five people were staying there," Scott laughed. "They were sleeping everywhere—in the bedrooms, in the basement, in the living room. We joked about buying an old motel to make room for everyone."

"Granny's house was a comfort zone," Sarah explained. "I didn't like leaving it."

On a couple of occasions Sarah did see a therapist at the hospital. However, her visits were short and she needed more in-depth counseling to cope with all she'd been through.

"We talked once for five minutes and once for twenty minutes. But he was asking me questions like, "Do you want to kill yourself?" I said, "Are you serious? I just protected my life and my baby's life. No, I don't want to kill myself."

Nevertheless, Sarah was clearly suffering from post traumatic stress disorder. This is an ailment which often inflicts individuals after they witness or are involved with traumatic events. Research on armed force members returning from the Vietnam War brought awareness to this condition. In reality, it has been around forever. It was just never understood, diagnosed or treated.

Sarah's mixed feelings caused her emotions to move from highs to lows and back again. She relived the attack on a daily basis. She felt she had been right to defend herself and her unborn baby, but she felt guilt that Katie died at her hand. In her words:

"It changes from day to day. Some days I feel happy McKaila Grace is healthy and bringing joy to our lives. Other days I think Katie Smith's life was so messed up that she'd try to kill me to get my baby and still other days I feel disgusted when I realize what her family has done to incense the whole police case and blame me."

Sarah was shocked and dismayed to learn some versions of what had happened between her and Katie as reported by some members of Katie Smith's family. And so it went, her emotions ricocheting from anger to joy to pain to fear to sorrow and back again. Nevertheless, she was always thankful her child had been saved. But this didn't stop her emotions from being erratic and traumatic.

Through it all, her entire family supported her. She had the love and strength of Scott, his family and her own. Sarah Brady's counseling records reveal a lot about her ordeal. A therapist noted on June 2, 2005:

"Sarah reported that she was involved in an incident where a lady tried to kill her to take her unborn baby and the other woman died in the incident. She said that she thought that she could handle it, because she was focused on the baby. Sarah said that as time goes by, she is struggling."

In the therapy assessment, it is noted that Sarah possessed the following strengths:
- history of emotional stability
- good cognitive skills
- sense of hope
- positive coping skills
- sense of humor
- religion/spirituality

However, the records also reflect Sarah was experiencing symptoms of stress: high anxiety, fear of being alone, panic attacks, fearfulness, tension, depression and decreased sleep. These symptoms escalated after her child was born. The therapist also remarked: "Client exhibits very cautious behavior, unable to come to agency without family member, family member needs to sit outside the therapist's office for support." The therapist also notes Sarah is "hyper vigilant."

In the hospital after her daughter was born, the doctor had prescribed tranquilizers, but Sarah stopped taking them after several weeks. The therapist now diagnosed Sarah with Post Traumatic Stress Disorder. At night Sarah tossed and turned from nightmares which involved being attacked in the same manner as she had on the frightening day Katie Smith had come after her with a knife. Prior to therapy, Sarah had *never* been to a psychiatrist, psychologist, or counseling for *any* condition prior to the Katie Smith attack.

"The therapist told me that not being able to stay home alone and the fear of going into public restrooms by myself were normal feelings."

Another counselor told Sarah she was progressing

better than expected.

"The counselor thought I was going to tell her I couldn't go out in public at all, couldn't go to Scott's son's basketball games, couldn't go to the grocery story," Sarah said. "But I have a family. I have a baby daughter and a stepson to care for. Certain things are still hard to do, but I have to get on with my life."

Once again, doctors placed Sarah on antidepressants; after a few weeks she quit taking them because they didn't seem to help much. Talking seemed to work better than anything, and one of the therapists at the clinic was very good at engaging Sarah in conversations about dealing with what had happened.

"We just talked and talked. I thought, this is exactly what I want and need to do. She told me to come back every week for a year, and I was looking forward to it."

But then the counselor presented a "plan of action." It was too regimented for Sarah. She just wanted to talk out how she was feeling that day or at that moment. The therapist's plan didn't leave much room for that, Sarah thought.

"She said, 'this is what we'll work on, this is what we'll talk about.' I said, 'No, that doesn't work for me. I might want to talk about something else.'" Eventually Sarah stopped going.

Sarah would still like to find a therapist or counselor whom she is comfortable talking with. "I can talk about this until I'm blue in the face. Just ask granny."

But she also appears to have come to grips with what happened that day in Fort Mitchell, when she took a life but saved her own and her unborn child.

"I had that period where I realized, I just killed

somebody. I know I did the right thing, but why did somebody have to die? I couldn't grasp why it happened. Now I've accepted that I don't know why it happened. I'll never know why it happened. But I don't feel as guilty; I don't feel as badly as I did right after I fought off the attack and killed Katie Smith. She gave me no choice. This was her fault. I only did what I had to do to save my baby."

Chapter 33

Seeds of Desperation

One of the ways women with very low self-esteem relating to family issues may look to satisfy such yearnings is to seek the unconditional love of a child. Katie Smith may have been searching for the love and affection absent from her own childhood.

Did Katie take on the Sarah Brody persona only to mislead Sarah Brady? Or was this simply an extension of the alternate self that Katie first revealed in high school? She might have desperately wanted to become someone else. It may have been Katie's way of escaping and coping with the reality of her dysfunctional childhood.

And often in her life, Katie seems to have indicated that her alcoholic parents were verbally abusive and degrading towards her. She may have internalized the criticism from her parents so deeply that she wanted to get away from her own persona and identity. Maybe attaining a baby of her own, she fantasized, would allow Katie to get control over what happened in her own family. Escaping into a new personality, lifestyle and family, as well as taking a new name, could have been Katie's way to create a new reality other than the desperate life she lived.

Abraham Maslow's Hierarchy of Needs Theory explains the natural desire to feel loved and needed. People "have a constant desire to feel needed. In the absence of these elements, people become increasingly susceptible to loneliness, social anxiety and depression." Katie Smith may have wanted a child of her own to care for in order to vicariously repair the damage done by her own emotionally unavailable parents. It's also possible that she was never truly able to have a childhood of her own and her imagination of a new existence with a child could recreate one.

It's not uncommon for lonely, emotionally upset teenagers or young single women (similar to Katie Smith) to want a child of their own. They may consider a baby a new beginning to their own life as well as the baby's. The epidemic of teenage pregnancy is widespread. According to recent Census data, by age twenty, thirty-five percent of girls get pregnant.

The National Campaign to Prevent Teen Pregnancy makes several valid observations:

"Compared to women who delay childbearing, teen mothers are less likely to complete high school and more likely to end up on welfare. The children of teen mothers are at significantly increased risk of low birth weight and prematurity, mental retardation, poverty, growing up without a father, welfare dependency, poor school performance, insufficient healthcare, inadequate parenting, and abuse and neglect."

However, the stigma associated with young unwed motherhood doesn't run as deeply in society as it did only years ago.

Recently, a 'pregnancy epidemic' occurred at Timken High School in Canton, Ohio. Several students became pregnant around the same time. According to viewers of the problem at the school, being pregnant at Timken High School isn't seen as being abnormal; instead it's considered a rite of passage.

In an article on the epidemic in *Seventeen* magazine, Lynette Doyle, a student at Timken High remarks, "I see girls at school bragging, saying, 'I think I might be pregnant,' just to get attention." Although the school board claims to have introduced an improved sex education program, student Monica Selby disagrees, stating, "Every day I ride the bus home and see more girls with babies and diaper bags. And they're getting younger—like twelve to fourteen."

Is this the result of insufficient sex education? Or could this be happening more frequently because it's considered trendy?

Either way, girls who crave motherhood probably see pregnancy as an instant entrée into the world of adulthood. This is especially true with a first pregnancy, which is considered a rite of passage into society. These young mothers-to-be receive much they crave: adult attention, baby showers, gifts, feelings of power and of course the possibility of boundless love. They may think they've left childhood behind and are finally able to become strong and autonomous individuals. But in reality, they aren't mature adults, they are children taking on adult responsibilities without the education or ability to carry them out.

One very different situation in regards to the desire for a child poses other questions and problems as well. Women who decide to start a family later in life face another set of obstacles.

Are women waiting too long to have children? Is it assumed that women past the age of forty are easily able to become pregnant with the aid of today's advanced medical technology? As a result, are they going to great lengths just to have a child?

Of course, it would be ideal to be financially stable and settled in with the perfect career before launching into motherhood. Unfortunately though, this utopian thought may in fact raise the statistics of problems in fertility and normal infants.

Although older women may have the maturity and life experience to raise a family, young women are physically able to do so, but don't necessarily posses the maturity. Both circumstances appear to have major pros and cons.

Author Nancy Gibbs explains, "Baby Specialists can do a lot to help a twenty-nine year old whose tubes are blocked or thirty-two year olds whose husbands have a low sperm count." Nevertheless, there are numerous failures to conceive.

Moreover, specialists aren't as capable when trying to aid less fertile older women. In the media we see pregnant actresses well past the age of forty. The notion of older women conceiving may appear easily attainable to the public. Nonetheless, the truth is that although there have been many breakthroughs and some success with in-vitro fertilization as well as other methods of aiding infertility, there isn't any promise that infertility therapy for women past childbearing years will succeed 100 percent of the time and, in fact, statistics on success are very low.

According to recent Census data, "childlessness has doubled in the past twenty years, so that one in five women between ages forty and forty-four is childless."

Could there be a correlation between recent fetus thefts and infertility?

Lisa Montgomery, the perpetrator in a case of fetus theft in Missouri, was thirty-six years old and had several children of her own prior to committing the attack. Peggy Jo Connor, offender in a Pennsylvania case, was thirty-eight years old and also had children. And Connor was no longer able to conceive.

Maybe the idea of not being able to become pregnant any longer propelled these women to the point of insanity where they were driven to kill for a baby. Did they feel powerless once they became infertile? It's possible that (much like teenagers who become pregnant by choice) they viewed being able to bear children as a source of strength and power. It's likely that they thought of an additional child as a way to control their unhealthy family situations. When, in reality, a stolen baby would destroy their lives as well as the lives of others and push them further away from the ideal family life and motherhood they so desperately craved.

Chapter 34

Kidnapping Before Birth

One of the questions the assault on Sarah Brady brings to mind is: Why are more pregnant women being attacked in efforts to rob them of their unborn children?

Just two months prior to Katie Smith attempting to murder Sarah to get Sarah's baby, a thirty-seven year-old woman named Lisa Montgomery began showing off her new baby boy to neighbors, family, friends, her pastor, even her unsuspecting husband.

But Montgomery, of Melvern, Kansas never gave birth to the baby boy. She had strangled his mother, Bobbie Jo Stinnet, twenty-three, of Skidmore, Missouri, removed the eight-month-old fetus who survived, and began caring for the baby as if it were her own. The FBI says Montgomery won Stinnet's trust over the Internet and through emails after Stinnet logged onto a rat terrier breeding Web site that Montgomery and her husband operated. As with Katie Smith, Montgomery had fooled everyone, prior to her deadly attack on Stinnet, into believing she was pregnant.

USA Today reported that the attack on Sarah Brady was the third assault on an expectant mother since 2003 and the ninth since 1987, according to National Center for Missing and Exploited Children in Alexandria, Virginia. Other attacks were in Oklahoma (2003), Ohio (2000), California (1998), Alabama (1996), Illinois (1995), Texas (1992) and New Mexico (1987). Experts who have studied the bizarre phenomenon said perpetrators are devious, calculating and bold. Their crimes are well-planned. In most cases the women abductors act alone. The FBI is studying the Katie Smith/Sarah Brady incident to better understand this type of bizarre crime. Sarah Brady has fully cooperated, giving hours of testimony.

"It's assumed that (the women) must be delusional," explained Cathy Nahirny, a supervisor at the center for Missing and Exploited Children. But they are also "very organized and quite rational. They follow a predictable pattern."

Researchers studied the established pattern for the first time in the 1987 New Mexico attack, the first recorded instance of what the Journal of Forensic Sciences would label "newborn kidnapping by Caesarean section." Women who launch such attacks possess a "childbearing fantasy" but are "cold, calculating and extremely self-centered," said Ann Burgess, a Boston College professor of nursing and the study's lead author.

In the New Mexico attack, Cindy Ray, eight months pregnant at the time, stood outside a prenatal clinic at

Kirtland Air Force base in Albuquerque when Darci Pierce, nineteen, offered her a ride.

Pierce, while faking a pregnancy and who previously told friends she had lost a child to a miscarriage, had a savage plan. With surgical tools and medical books waiting at her home, she choked Ray unconscious before reaching her house. To Pierce's surprise, when she dashed up to the house she saw her husband was home. So Pierce drove the pregnant Ray out to an isolated area in the New Mexico desert. There, Pierce tied Ray to a tree and, in a ghoulish and horrific procedure, used her car keys to perform a macabre Caesarean delivery on Ray.

Pierce delivered a baby girl who lived; Ray bled to death.

Police arrested Pierce after her attempt to obtain a birth certificate at a hospital. An exam indicated she had not recently delivered a baby. Convicted, but found mentally ill, she is serving thirty years in prison.

In another frightening incident, Debra Evans, twenty-eight, let Levern Ward into her Addison, Illinois, home in November of 1995. The pregnant Evans once dated Ward. However, he had abused her and a court ordered him to stay away from her.

Once inside, Ward, twenty-four, his cousin, Jacqueline Annette Williams, twenty-eight, and her boyfriend, Fedell Caffey, went on a senseless killing spree. Caffey shot Evans in the head, then he and Ward stabbed Evans' ten year old daughter to death.

While still in Evans' home, the trio performed a crude Caesarean on Evans and fled with the baby. Caffey later called a cousin and told him "he had just had a son."

Later, Williams and Caffey slit the throat of Evans' seven year-old son and dumped his body ten miles from his house.

Caffey, Williams and Ward were charged with murder and kidnapping.

Margarita Flores, forty, and Josephine Sonia Sultana, forty, met in a Southern California hospital. Flores, who suffered from diabetes and uterine cancer, received treatment; Sultana worked as a translator. At the time, Flores was eight and a half months pregnant.

In September 1998 Sultana used a devious method similar to Katie Smith's promise of baby gifts. Sultana called Flores and told her she had free baby furniture and a one-year supply of diapers. They just needed to go to a nearby warehouse to pick up the gifts.

Later in the day, witnesses saw the two women arguing in the parking lot of a restaurant. Flores was never seen again, though parts of her body were found in a trash can in Tijuana, Mexico. Her baby had been cut from her womb.

Two days after being convicted of murder and kidnapping, Sultana hung herself with a sheet in her jail cell.

All these cases have occurred in the past ten years prompting mental health professionals and the law enforcement community as well as the media to search for common motives and personality characteristics. Jonathan Stoudmire, a forensic psychiatrist at Cincinnati's University Hospital, said in some cases women can be driven to commit fetal abductions because of a past event, such as child abuse, which is what Katie Smith had claimed. Experts call it factitious disorder.

"People who suffer from factitious disorder get satisfaction from taking the role of a sick person," Stoudmire told The *Kentucky Post*. "Being pregnant is almost like that. You get a lot of attention when you're pregnant.

"People with these types of disorders often have something traumatic happen to them when they were younger. If she indeed was molested by her father, that relationship was shot and she had a huge void in her life."

Sarah Brady's ordeal is unique in one fortunate aspect. She is believed to be one of only three women to ever survive attacks to extract a baby from a pregnant woman, according to the National Center for Missing and Exploited Children. In addition, she's the only woman who killed her attacker and survived.

ABC News reported that homicide was a leading cause of death among pregnant women in the United States between 1991 and 1999, according to a March 2005 study published in *The American Journal of Public Health*.

The Centers for Disease Control and Prevention (CDC) Pregnancy Mortality Surveillance System found that the pregnancy-associated homicide ratio was 1.7 per 100,000 lives births.

Experts such as Pat Brown, a profiler and Chief Executive Officer of The Pat Brown Criminal Profiling Agency, said most pregnant women are killed by men who see the pregnancy and unborn child as obstacles and burdens in their lives.

"The usual reason when it involves a man is the

(unborn) baby," Brown told ABC. "The baby is causing a complication in his life."

Brown cited the highly publicized case of Scott Peterson, the California man convicted of killing his pregnant wife, Laci, and the unborn son they planned to allegedly name Conner, so he could continue his extramarital affair with Amber Frey.

Women's motivations in attacks on expectant mothers are often more complicated and rooted deeper in psychosis.

"Women who actually want to steal a woman's baby are usually psychopaths," Brown reported. "They claim to be pregnant when they are not. She usually loves the attention and power that is associated with pregnancy and motherhood. They like to use the child to get attention for themselves. But they like to try to manipulate others with the issues that motherhood and pregnancy bring."

Katie's devious plan to lure Sarah to her apartment is actually part of a pattern used by women intent on stealing babies, according to a story by The *Kentucky Enquirer.*

The newspaper quoted John Raburn, a vice president and chief operating officer of the National Center for Missing and Exploited Children. He has studied more than 200 cases of newborn abductions since 1984.

Raburn drew a portrait of the typical fetus attacker.

"They are women of childbearing age," he told *The Kentucky Enquirer*. "They are slightly overweight. They are incredibly good at lying, manipulating and conning, and in most cases have grown up that way. And they've done some nesting, so they've bought a crib and diapers."

The *Kentucky Enquirer* also consulted a 2002 study of newborn kidnapping by Caesarean section published in the *Journal of Forensic Sciences*.

"The female abductors, in essence, become a mother by proxy by acting out a fantasy of them delivering a baby," according to the study. "It becomes the way she can feel it is her baby to bond with and to ensure she would be the first mother image to the baby. This Caesarean section fantasy differs from other cases in which violence is used because it is not just getting the baby, but to assume the mothering ability in producing the baby."

Brown dispels the notion that women who attack or kill pregnant women are failed mothers or are grieving because of past miscarriages or failed attempted pregnancies.

"This is not a matter of grieving," he said. "They are liars. They've usually had histories of lying about being pregnant. And they have to be a pretty cold-blooded killer to kill a pregnant woman."

Another attempt to steal a pregnant woman's child followed Sarah's ordeal. As reported by the *Pittsburgh Post-Gazette*, in October 2005, Peggy Jo Conner attempted to kill Valerie Oskin and steal her unborn child. The event happened in Ford City, Pennsylvania, in Armstrong County. Peggy Jo Connor and Valerie Oskin lived next to each other. Peggy Jo had three children from prior marriages. She informed her boyfriend at the time and others, she was pregnant. Like Katie Smith, she stocked her home with newborn necessities such as baby carriers and clothes. Peggy Jo fooled everyone, claiming seven months of pregnancy.

Living in a trailer park in Pattonsville, neighbors reported to the press that Peggy Jo stayed at home to care for her children and never showed any sign of a propensity for violence. She befriended Valerie Oskin who has a young son and was eight months pregnant.

Police reported Peggy Jo hit Valerie with a baseball bat and placed Valerie and Valerie's unharmed son in her car. After dropping the boy off with family, she drove to Wayne Township close to Rural Valley. While Valerie was still alive, Peggy Jo opened her stomach with a razor knife. (Peggy Jo's claimed seven to eight month pregnancy coincides with the national publicity of Katie Smith's attack on Sarah Brady.) Was Peggy Jo imitating Katie Smith?

Adam Silvis, only seventeen, was out driving a four wheeler when he stumbled upon Peggy Jo's macabre plan in the woods. He saw Peggy Jo standing over Valerie and heard Valerie's cries of pain. Adam went home, told his father of his discovery and they contacted the police.

The police came to the scene and directed Valerie to be transported to Allegheny General Hospital. Valerie and her child, taken by emergency C-section, survived. During her recovery, Valerie confirmed Peggy Jo as her attacker. Police recovered a bat, razor edge, "birthing kit" and other evidence of the plan of Peggy Jo Conner.

The prosecutor has charged Peggy Jo Conner with attempted homicides.

The Fort Mitchell Police cooperated with the FBI in studying the Brady case to help profile future attackers of pregnant women intending to steal their unborn children. Sarah did her part. She authorized the release of her detailed transcript and statement to the police. The FBI finished their review. The police have turned their file over to the prosecutor in Kenton County, Kentucky, Bill Crockett.

It was now up to Bill Crockett to decide whether to take the matter to a grand jury or to close the case.

The FBI's case analysis held that Katie Smith had the motivation, ability and opportunity to lure Sarah Brady to her residence for the purpose of incapacitating or killing Sarah Brady and then delivering and abducting her baby to raise as her own child.

The motivation involved in this case, known as "infant replacement," can be defined as the motivation to obtain a child based upon the offender's own maternal desires.

Though each case differs, the offenders all possess similar motivations and personality traits to those of Katie Smith.

Chapter 35

The Price of a Child

The frightening attack on Sarah Brady's fetus leads to another terrifying query. Are children becoming an even higher commodity in today's society than they were years previously? Adoption, in-vitro fertilization, egg donation, surrogate parenting and, unfortunately, the black market, are several ways in which men and women who desperately want to parent are able to acquire children in today's world.

It's very unlikely that the story the Smith family alleged in regards to Sarah Brady's intention to sell her baby to Katie Smith is true. Why would she sell her child for as little as $5,000 as claimed?

The black market remains a notorious choice for many individuals who are unable to conceive or adopt and have become frustrated. According to author M. Haviland, babies have been sold on the black market since the 1920s, due to the lack of orphanages operated by the state. Black market adoption allowed babies to be sold to prospective parents interested in adoption.

Several documented groups of black market babies as noted by Haviland include, "Cole babies, Hicks babies, Bessie babies, Dr. Mary babies, Butterbox babies and Springer babies."

Haviland explains that infants were sold "from elite maternity homes to the back doors of private doctors' offices, babies began to be sold in great numbers by unscrupulous doctors, attorneys, and other individuals."

Anyone was able to buy a child, no inquiries, waiting lists or applications needed. Though immoral, frustrated couples sometimes resorted to this route. Haviland states that in the 1920s, children sold for as little as one-hundred dollars and as much as ten-thousand dollars. Although the black market trade for children was not a secret industry, no measures were taken to prevent it from expanding into a larger business.

Various methods were used by sellers to obtain infants from single mothers unable to raise them. Haviland explains how unwed pregnant women would often opt to stay with a doctor for a fee until she delivered her child, at which point the doctor would sell the infant to a couple. The women were generally unaware that their babies were being sold. The doctor would then provide false information noting the 'new' parents as the birth parents on a counterfeit birth certificate. Though many of the adoptive parents were benevolent and caring people, some individuals weren't fit to become parents (since there wasn't any precautionary background screening done).

There are countless individuals desperate to find out who their birth parents are and if they have siblings of whom they are unaware of due to an earlier separation. Since the documents created for these individuals are false, the adoptive parents remain the only possible source of background information for adoptees.

One posting on geocities.com shows only a photograph of an unnamed woman with the following caption, "I am a black market adoptee and I have spent the past sixteen years in search of information that could lead me to the answers for questions that are burning deep inside of me. Although I have been able to gather volumes of information, very few facts are known today."

Writer Ethan B. Kapstein states, "Children are our most precious resource—and, like most precious resources, they are traded across borders. As more parents have adopted babies from abroad over the past decade, the international market for children has boomed: in 2001, some 34,000 children—mainly from Asia and central and eastern Europe—found new homes in western Europe and North America."

Kapstein explains that because millions of children are suffering in third-world orphanages, the chances of creating caring families interested in international adoption has increased significantly over the years. He states that putting a ban on adoption "from countries that tolerate corrupt adoption rings is no solution either."

Abortion and birth control have also increased the demand for adoptable infants. However, the West possesses the high demand for these children, while third world countries have the highest population of unwanted babies. As a result, the Chinese black market baby trade appears to have grown significantly over the years.

According to author Lynne O'Donnell, "In a country where families place a premium on boys and most people are restricted to having one child to conform with draconian population control measures, the market for stolen babies is booming."

O'Donnell expands on this point, stating that babies are not only stolen from families, but are sometimes bred for sale. O'Donnell explains that because the Chinese "government closes bankrupt and insufficient mines and increases the use of natural gas, migrant workers, who number more than 200 million nationwide, are resorting to crime to make money."

Because these children are able to be sold for a large sum, former migrant workers resort to becoming involved in the black market baby trade. O'Donnell states that the average rural income is a mere one hundred thirty-six dollars per month, and baby boys can be bought for up to three thousand two hundred eighty dollars.

According to a Beijing police report in 2006, "People involved with the adoption of Chinese children by foreigners have long worried that parents might unknowingly receive children who were abducted or stolen from their families. They worry that accusations of baby trafficking could lead officials to limit or stop the process that has given homes to thousands of Chinese children who might otherwise grow up in orphanages. Foreign parents often pay thousands of dollars in fees or donations to adoption agencies or orphanages."

In recent years, the utilization of the World Wide Web has allowed the black market baby trade to become more accessible internationally.

On one particular website, orphans from around the world are advertised for sale. Author Debora L. Spars states that prices per child vary, depending on health, race and age. Spars notes that the cost to adopt a teenager from foster care in the United States tends to be very inexpensive. However, she explains that a "healthy white Russian infant" generally costs over $35,000. Spars states that a photograph and a brief description explaining each child's interests and dreams of the future are posted on one website.

Although millions of unwanted children are in desperate need of families to call their own, is the black market or private adoption the best means for them? They have no say in the matter and their family lives are left entirely to chance. These children may be lucky and land in families of caring, wonderful parents, or they may find themselves at the mercy of unscrupulous individuals. More stringent laws and regulations are needed to regulate this gray area for the benefit of the children whose futures are at stake.

Chapter 36

Unsolicited Aftereffects

Well over a year after Katie Smith's attack, Sarah Brady was still trying to put the ordeal behind her. Unfortunately, people still gawk. One particular startling incident occurred when Sarah's sister had a chance encounter with a member of Katie Smith's family at a restaurant in Covington. It was an awkward, even frightening moment.

"I'm so fearful that one day I'm going to run into one of these people from her family that think I supposedly sold her my baby and then killed her," Sarah said. "I'm still worried about it, very worried about it."

There have been many other disturbing moments. One day in a laundromat a man was staring at Sarah and Mckaila Grace making Sarah very uncomfortable with his persistent gaze. When the man approached Sarah, her mother, who had met her at the laundromat, stood between him and the baby.

Sarah said, "He came up yelling, 'Is that the girl from

Fort Mitchell? Is that the baby that lived?' We looked at him like there was something wrong with him."

But then the man approached Sarah's mother and continued to ask questions about Sarah and the baby.

He then started babbling things about them he'd read in the papers and on television.

"What really frightened me were the details he had memorized," Sarah said. "He knew her name, knew my name and knew where I lived. That stuff is scary. He said, 'Can I have your new address so I can have our church pray for you?' Of course I said no. But he wouldn't leave us alone, and the laundry attendant finally called the police."

However, the man left before the police arrived. The police basically told Sarah they could obviously not prevent these incidents.

Sarah sighed heavily, "Wherever we go people stop and stare, say things, ask me questions. That happens at least once a week. People come up to us and say, 'Well, how is Mckaila?' People I don't even know speak to us."

How long will it go on? Sarah wonders. Will Mckaila have to deal with gawkers, stalkers, reporters and the memory of what happened on that February day in Fort Mitchell? Sarah hopes not, but she frankly doesn't know.

Sarah had intended to return to work after the birth of Mckaila Grace. Now, she refuses to leave her daughter at a daycare center or with a babysitter.

"After what's happened, I won't allow it."

Though time has passed, Sarah has trouble being alone. Her mother visits her daily. She will not use public restrooms. Mckaila Grace is never out of her sight.

"I'm panicked in closed off spaces," Sarah said. "The psychologist, therapist, whatever she is, said it was very normal to react that way because of what I've been through. She said most people who suffer post traumatic stress syndrome won't even go out in public.

"As time goes on I'm improving. As long as Mckaila is with me, I'll go to a restaurant, I'll go into a store," she said. "Actually, I'm more comfortable being out in public than I am being in closed places. I always need members of my family accompanying me."

Sarah even insisted on having a family member at her side while her gallbladder was being removed.

"I specifically told my doctor, I will not go back to the hospital by myself to get prepped (for surgery) unless I have a family member with me," she said.

But the hospital staff refused. Sarah began sobbing when she was taken into a room by herself and the doors closed.

"The nurse came back in and said, 'What's wrong?' And I had to tell her the story. She got nervous, because on my file there was a note saying, 'Be cautious. You know, kind of handle her with kid gloves because she's been through a lot.' She became red in the face and she started fluttering around me asking me if I was sure I was alright. And I wasn't."

"I freaked out in that room with that door shut," Sarah said. "So they had to go back and get Scott."

Recovering from the surgery, Sarah spent that summer trying to accustom herself to the tasks of being a new mother. Like many parents she had to act used to the sleep depravation that often accompanies mothering a newborn.

"She's not a sleeper," Sarah says of her daughter. "Not at all, but she disarms us with her smiles and gurgles."

Scott's son has become a doting big brother. He's also his little sister's most ardent guardian.

"He's great with her. Scott's son picks her up; he takes care of her. He says, 'Sarah, can I take her in my room and sit her on the bed so she can watch sports with me since she likes baseball?'

"He shows her off to all of his friends. One day when I brought him to school he asked me to let him take Mckaila, and told me I should go to his classroom. To my surprise, the kids collected money and bought a baby gift when Scott's son told them all about the cute things his baby sister was doing."

"He was taking her around showing his sister to everybody, and he was just ecstatic, saying things like, 'doesn't she look like me and my dad? She doesn't look like Sarah; she looks like us.' Yeah, he's very proud of his sister, and he's very protective of her."

And the baby is lovely and loving. Who can blame him?

"We all shudder when we think how a disturbed woman with a troubled past tried to split his family by killing me, the woman he knows as his stepmother, and taking the baby sister he may have never known. Well, she didn't succeed and I look in the mirror and I know that I did the right thing."

Although Sarah has dealt with many hardships throughout her life, she now feels that somehow all the tribulations she endured built up her courage so it was there when she needed it most. She had the strength to save not only her life, but for her most importantly, Mckaila Grace's. As Sarah says, "Everything has turned out just fine."

Epilogue

Sarah discusses the effect the Katie Smith attack had on her life in her own words:

"The most disturbing part of the whole disastrous event is how it not only affected me, but others as well. I watched people close to me deal with the reality that they almost lost Mckaila Grace and me. If this evil plan had been successful, my daughter would be at the hands of a psychotic. Who really knows what she would have done with my daughter if I had died and she had lived. The terrifying dreams of this being a reality give me cold chills. They burn a hollowness right through my stomach into my very being. I feel hollow at the idea of a crazy person raising my child. I have observed my friends getting angry when we walk into a restaurant and hear people whisper things about me being "the lady who killed her attacker." I had to watch the torment in my stepson's eyes as we were at a local bowling alley, and the people next to us kept trying to get a glimpse of his sister, staring and pointing. And we all endure the ongoing fear that someone else may want to hurt us. I want my family to be free from any more anguish the attack may have caused them. I want them to know that I eventually will be okay.

"And there are troubling little things as well. The dismay that we have that I'm unable to have my daughter's picture taken because we are afraid the media will get a hold of it and someone out there unbalanced like Katie Smith may see it and come after her. There are only snapshots for us to show her of her first few days of life. Many of the rights she deserved have been stripped from Mckaila Grace. She wasn't able to bond with her mother at home right after she was born, something most mothers and infants don't even question. We couldn't even return to our homes because of the case glaring in the media spotlight. My daughter's birth had made national news. Even today I can't sit down to do her baby book without anxiety; her mementos of the first few months of her life bring back all the terror of that horrific day.

"And my own life has changed. I no longer have that privacy that each individual deserves. I watch as Scott and I struggle financially, because we are too afraid to leave our child with anyone, so that I can go back to work. The fear that seems almost unthinkable really happened to us. We can't take that chance again. Scott has tried even harder to make us stay afloat, struggling through all these hardships. I watch as he has been beaten down by my emotional state, while trying to deal with his own emotions.

"Scott's mom had to leave work, because so many

people were singling her out, flooding her with questions, wanting to know the whole story. She was unable to deal with the stress in her own way. Scott's Granny and Pappy had to open their homes up to our whole family. They had the media hounding at their door and the phone. This is a time in their life when they are retired and should be relaxing and relishing in the love of children and grandchildren, instead they are fighting to help keep us safe and secure. My mom has health problems all related to stress. Her Crohn's Disease has become worse since all of this happened. All the pain swirls within me, making me question why all this unnecessary unhappiness has been put on those I love. Trying to deal with all this blame I have put on myself becomes somewhat mentally exhausting. I try to think of ways that I can ease all of their lives. The bottom line is there is no way to change the events of that terrible day. They will be forever branded in our hearts and minds. Every day brings a new set of feelings. As of yet, I really haven't found a way to deal with all the issues; nevertheless, I am hopeful that with time things will become easier for everyone.

"And yet my family is surviving and coming through our period of pain and turmoil. We all receive "therapy" through the love of my daughter, Mckaila Grace. I have found out through all of the torment, there was good. I have become closer to my family. We have all come together as one. My survival and that of my tiny daughter has made an impression on people all around the world. I have received letters, cards and gifts expressing gratitude from complete strangers. All of them let me know how fearless they feel I was.

"Part of me continues to struggle with all the anguish. I still have my angry days, but they are becoming less frequent as time passes. Sometimes, I still feel anger toward Katie and her family. But I want to get past all those evil spirits that continue to haunt me. I can't help but blame Katie for all the destruction she caused. But I do realize they are hurdles that I have to overcome. Nevertheless, I face apprehension with every stranger I meet. My heart beats loudly and hard when I see someone who has an uncanny resemblance to Katie Smith. I can't stay at home by myself. I worry that something horrible could happen again and I won't be able to protect myself. Katie has robbed me of all of my purity. I have panic attacks. I fear that someone who loved Katie will seek out vengeance. These are concerns I deal with every day.

"My encounter with Katie has damaged me. I not only place blame on Katie, but also on the members of her family that have helped drag out the police investigation. I realize that they had a death to mourn; however, they didn't have to unleash havoc on an innocent victim. Anyone who was aware of Katie's delusions fed into her demented state of mind and neither helped her nor came forward to protect others. They ignored the signs and chose not to interfere as she led a life of deception. She preyed on their link as a family but they ignored the troubling signs of mental instability.

"It makes me sad to know that there was a possibility her death and attempt on my life possibly could have been avoided. If one person had taken a stand to help this woman instead of encouraging her erratic behavior, all the tragic events that played out could have been avoided. Katie was a woman who needed serious professional help, and no one helped her get it. It was easier to be a player in her fantasy life, than a martyr who could help save her. Maybe it was the fact no one wanted to be bothered or no one cared enough. These questions I pose to myself on a regular basis may never get answered. I have to come to terms that this part of the horrific experience is not my problem. I am not the person who will eternally wonder whether or not there was anything I could have done to help her.

"There is one person that I do think will have guilt lingering over her head for a long time. The supposed doctor who testified in Katie's father trial—one who said Katie was credible and felt she was suffering from repressed memory syndrome. This is a woman whose credentials were investigated and found deficient, a very sad scenario for Katie that a therapist would allow her cries for help to go unanswered. All of this just to help convict a man who may be innocent, a man who appears not to have received a fair trial. Katie's father not only had an ill-prepared attorney, an alleged doctor for the prosecution, but his accuser was his daughter who was far from credible. She was a woman who had led a life of deceit, fantasy relationships and imagined diseases. How could any man receive a trial with justice, with all these factors infecting his defense? I can't make a determination of his proclaimed innocence, but I do feel that he was not given the fairness of being considered innocent before proven guilty. As I watched the special Channel Five show in regards to the appeal Tim Smith was granted because of all of the revelations, a part of me seethed anger. Now his conviction has been overturned and I feel somehow relieved, and hope justice has been served.

"These traumatic events have brought enormous turmoil, but I have tried to confront and cope with it all. I have come to the conclusion that the fateful day in February will be with me for the rest of my life. But I haven't come to the realization that I have to quit allowing my self to sponge up all the bad and none of the good. I have decided to try and take all the new and old positive aspects of my life and concentrate on the present. Once I took and passed the lie detector test, I came to the conclusion that I could get past all of this. I am now concentrating on life's positive attributes.

"I have a beautiful daughter and son who deserve to have a complete mother. I want to be someone who can share all their light, laughter and innocence of life. All of these were attacked on February 10, 2005, but I am making strides as I fill my heart again with the joys of family.

"I now know, perhaps in part in coming through all this anguish, I am a strong woman who deserves her second chance at life. I will prevail healthy and be whole again. All of this will take time. I am not completely healed, but I am on the road to recovery. The joyful sight of the children in my life, not only my own, but my nieces and nephews, show me there is so much to live for. There is a brighter future and all my days won't be filled with haunting pictures of Katie and that frightful day. I will conquer the inner demons that at times wrack my heart and soul. God is always there for me to talk to and reassure me that my life has a purpose.

"Above all I have learned there have been many things that have come out of this whole account that are optimistic and promising. I am grasping that there is so much to life that I had not appreciated before. I lived a wonderful life before all of this, but I have a newfound admiration for pieces of my life that I didn't realize were so important before. I am starting to build a foundation with my father, one that had not existed before. We are trying to fill the holes that have been missing for a long time. Scott and I no longer worry ourselves with trivial fights. We appreciate the small gifts in life. Nothing is too minuscule; everything makes a difference. I have learned to savor and appreciate every day. Most people only get one shot at life; it is well worth enjoying.

"I want to share my story with others. As I read through all the stories of other women whose unborn babies were attacked and who didn't survive, my heart aches for the families. I know each victim is in heaven with God and can no longer be harmed. They are watching over their families and keeping them safe. I hope the victims' families know how brave and strong their daughters, mothers, wives, sisters, aunts, cousins, whoever they may be, fought for the most sacred thing in the world, their child. The children who survived the attack need to know how blessed their lives are. Each and every one of them is a miracle. Every child that is born is a miracle, but these children are extra special.

"I want to tell those who don't appreciate the gift of life that each day they should wake up and thank God to be alive. Our time on earth is supposed to be spent relishing every minute of the day, not allowing the evil to break us down. My encounter with evil has given me the willpower to survive. I want to help victims of trauma. I want to speak out against the women who think they can make this type of violence a part of our everyday lives, because they are wrong. I am now proud of what I have done. I prevailed over a person who sought to take everything from me and my family. We have to put a stop to such horrible crimes. I want people to gain something positive from my story of triumph over evil.

"I still have days when I am tempted to sink back into the depression and sorrow, but I watch the eyes of my daughter light up with joy and I go forward. I watch my stepson become so intense and determined to accomplish so many things; I know that this is what life is all about. If I become upset or sad, I now pick up the phone and talk to someone. Talking about all of my problems and fears is a crucial part of the healing process. There is a very long road ahead of me, but I feel with the closing of the case, proper therapy and sharing my stories with others, I will eventually reach my destination. Grace and the goodness of others have helped me through all the pain and suffering, and will help me to continue on. My family support system will never fade and for that I will be indebted to them for the rest of my life. I can never express my gratitude for all the goodwill that has been bestowed upon me. There is no way to thank everyone for everything they have done for Mckaila Grace and me. But I will move forward with the grace of God."

Update—
Saving Grace

Friday, April 29, 2006 proved to be a landmark day in the Sarah Brady and Katie Smith story.

Bill Crockett, the Kenton County Commonwealth Attorney, and the Fort Mitchell Police Department closed the case against Sarah Brady. Scott Nottingham, the Fort Mitchell Police Detective, appeared before a grand jury and presented his department's findings and conclusions. He also answered all questions from Bill Crockett and the grand jury. The grand jury decided that Sarah Brady did not commit a crime.

"Sarah is happy and relieved that this part of it is all over. Even though it was a foregone conclusion in her mind, it's still comforting to know that now it's official. Technically, she was still the subject of a possible murder investigation, which would be terrifying for anybody. She had fully cooperated with the police. Based on her cooperation and the information they shared with us, it was clear to us there were not going to be charges," stated her attorney, Eric Deters.

According to Sergeant Tom Loos, the Fort Mitchell Police Department spent more time on their investigation than any other in at least the past eighteen years. Sergeant Loos confidently expressed that all leads and possibilities were thoroughly investigated. The police investigation included exploring the Smith family allegation that Sara Brady intended to sell her baby to Katie Smith. According to Sergeant Loos, the Smith family still has concerns. Eric Deters referred to the allegations as a "bunch of baloney" and pointed to Sarah's cooperation, the evidence, and the fact that she passed both a lie detector and voice analysis test.

"Sarah isn't guilty. She was simply defending herself. It is unfortunate Katie had to die, but she obviously needed help which she never received," said Katie Smith's cousin. Katie's cousin claimed that while in court, Katie admitted fabricating molestation charges against her father.

While the case against Sarah Brady was now closed, the battle involving Tim Smith's conviction continued. On the same date the grand jury failed to indict Sarah, Bill Crockett appealed Judge Patricia Summe's order overturning Tim Smith's conviction.

Pleas to the Kentucky Court of Appeals normally take a year or two. Melanie Lowe of the Kentucky Innocence Project said Tim Smith's defense team, led by Bill Lamb, was considering asking Judge Summe to set a bond for his release pending the appeal.

046572799